RESTLESS

BECAUSE YOU WERE MADE FOR MORE

AN EIGHT-SESSION BIBLE STUDY

JENNIE ALLEN

Harper*Christian*
Resources

Restless Study Guide
© 2013 by Jennie Allen

Published in Grand Rapids, Michigan, by HarperChristian Resources. HarperChristian Resources is a registered trademark of HarperCollins Christian Publishing, Inc.

Requests for information should be sent to customercare@harpercollins.com.

ISBN 978-0-849-92236-7 (softcover)
ISBN 978-0-849-92246-6 (ebook)

HarperChristian Resources titles may be purchased in bulk for church, business, fundraising, or ministry use. For information, please e-mail ResourceSpecialist@ChurchSource.com.

Typesetting: Crosslin Creative
Author image © Jessica Taylor. Used with permission.

First Printing December 2013 / Printed in the United States of America

CONTENTS

ACKNOWLEDGMENTS

There is an order to this type of thing: first God and then family and so on. But as you know, this project was built around moments that life changed forever because of Sarah Henry.

Sarah, you have changed everything about life. It can't go back for you, and it will never go back for us. We have watched you face death and days worse than death, and you still glow with a faith that transcends any earthly understanding.

There must be a God, because instead of shaking your fist, you have taught me to trust and love him more. You are brave, and I want to lean into the story God has for me the way you have, mighty friend. I love you.

Now to the others:

God, what a lovely sense of humor you have. I fight you, unsure every moment, and yet through the pain of it all, you give me what I need. Thank you for allowing me to be a little part of your story. You have the best, greatest story that could ever be imagined and it is an honor to build with you for it.

Zac, my love, thank you for being a man who pushes me to dream and obey. I love your sacrifice and protection of me. God gave me the best teammate on earth. You run faster than me, and yet you never leave me behind. I love you so.

To my kids: as I watch the threads of your lives begin to come together for great purposes, I want you to know we admire you so. You, my tribe of awesome people, are changing the world.

Conner, somewhere in the midst of these words you became a young man, and I love the man you are becoming. Your passion and strength are contagious and you light up our family with your mop of blond hair and sinister smile. I am proud that you are my son; and with your sharp mind, you will build great things so others prosper. I can't wait to see how.

Kate, you just get it. You get God and people and compassion in the deepest places in your soul. You crave all the right things: mercy and more of God and loving people. All of that mixed with your way with words and creativity will come together to impact people's souls. I see your threads, and they are already building the best stories.

Caroline, I love that pajamas and cuddling are enough for you to be happy every day. You bring a passionate joy to our home; you won't let us all miss each other. You are only eight, and you are one of the hardest workers I know. I think it is because you love beauty—the kind of beauty that comes from tables set with cloth napkins. You are winsome and kind, and many will want your God because of the way you love and serve.

Cooper, at six years old no one wonders if you will change the world. You will. You have. You charge into a room, into our lives, with authority and direction. There are no strangers, and your curiosity causes us all to wonder at God. You are a leader, and I envision the many lives that the threads of your story will impact.

And to the women who went to the hard places with me as *Restless* was taking shape in Austin: you made me believe God could use this work, these words. You were brave, and you live beautiful lives with unique threads. Thank you for investing in this with me.

To the friends in Austin who became sisters this year, thank you for cheering and praying and speaking life into my weary bones. I don't remember life without our text-stream sisterhood. And to Annie Downs: you made me believe I could write on empty and that God would come through. He did. Love you forever.

Many of these words were processed and written in a space that Cecil Eager graciously carved out for me. Cecil runs the Gruene Mansion Inn, a bed and breakfast in Gruene, Texas. And after many long, lonely nights of writing in the most ideal little writing cabin an hour from home, I would walk in for an obscene feast of a breakfast and he would be there with his warm smile and coffee and he would sit with me. Because that is what he does in Gruene. Cecil, your lifetime of threads have woven into a beautiful story and calling. Everything about the space you have created slows the soul.

I needed my soul to slow so that I could write these words. So readers, if you ever stop by this heavenly place, be sure to thank him for me.

And to the teams of people who believed in this enough to give their time and money and hearts to it, thank you. Curtis Yates, I can't imagine how much time you have spent on me in our brief relationship. Thank you for taking me on. I know you now feel brave for such an endeavor! Thank you for always thinking I am crazy and then helping me be crazy anyway. You are much more than an agent—you and Karen are dear friends.

Debbie Wickwire, you lost sleep with me over these words. You reminded me why we all do this, and you showed me God—you feel more like family than an editor. Thank you. To Matt Baugher, Emily Sweeney, Jana Muntsinger, Pamela McClure, Jennifer McNeil, Adria Haley, John Raymond, Robin Phillips, Mark Weising, Chris Fann, Greg Clouse, Sarah Johnson, and the countless others who broke molds with me and gave too much time to this project, your threads are as much a part of shaping this as mine. Thank you for believing in me and in this. Wouldn't it be fun if God took these efforts and unleashed people to his purposes on earth? I pray he does, and I hope you feel a big part of it!

Thanks also to Jessica Honneger and jewelry from Noonday Collection. To Greg Kwedar and team at Yarn Creative for being so creative and giving so much to these projects. To Courtney Landers and Mercury Hall in Austin, Texas, and to Scott Hill and Foundry Company.

Special thanks to my friends Monica Smith, Laura Choy, and Katie Henry for the time and work they did to build an incredible experience at Mercury Hall, and to all the amazing friends who were a part of filming this project. Their voices and prayers have shaped it.

Again, so grateful to all of you! I am blessed.

Jennie

INSTRUCTIONS AND EXPECTATIONS

WHAT DO YOU HOPE TO GET OUT OF THIS STUDY?

_____

_____

_____

_____

GET HONEST

This is going to get personal, but it will be worth it. We will be dealing with the very things that make you, you. God wants to do something with those things. But until we recognize that we are made to run a race all our own, we will miss what he has for us. If you consider yourself restless, perhaps you would be willing to consider a way out, even if it is costly. Be honest with yourself and honest with God. He knows all of it anyway.

ENGAGE WITH YOUR SMALL GROUP

An important part of personal growth is community. We are going to deal with the way we view God and how we are to spend our lives individually for him. You may even need time outside of this small group to process with others your passions and gifts and purpose. Be intentional to pursue deeper conversations with others through this process.

And you shall know the truth, and the truth shall make you free.

JOHN 8:32 NKJV

COMMIT TO BEING CONSISTENT AND PRESENT

Commit to being present at your group meetings, barring an emergency, and arrange your schedule so you do not miss any part in this journey. Have your lesson and projects finished when you come to the group meeting (except for this first one, of course).

GROUND RULES FOR GROUP DISCUSSION TIME

BE CONCISE.

Share your answers to the questions while protecting others' time for sharing. Be thoughtful. Don't be afraid to share with the group, but try not to dominate the conversation.

> Let every person be quick to hear, slow to speak.
>
> **JAMES 1:19** ESV

KEEP GROUP MEMBERS' STORIES CONFIDENTIAL

Many things your group members share are things they are choosing to share with you, not with your husband or other friends. Protect each other by not allowing anything shared in the group to leave the group.

RELY ON SCRIPTURE FOR TRUTH

We are prone to use conventional, worldly wisdom as truth. While there is value in that, this is not the place. If you feel led to respond, please only respond with God's truth and Word, not "advice."

NO COUNSELING

Protect the group by not directing all attention on solving one person's problem. This is the place for confessing and discovery and applying truth together as a group. Your group leader will be able to direct you to more help outside the group time if you need it. Don't be afraid to ask for help.

STUDY DESIGN

In the first meeting, your groups' study guides will be passed out and you will work through the Introduction lesson together. After that, each lesson in the study guide is meant to be completed on your own during the week before coming to the group meeting. These lessons may feel different from studies you have done in the past. They are very interactive. The beginning of each lesson will involve you, your Bible, and a pen, working through Scripture and listening to God's voice. Each lesson will conclude with four projects you can do to help you further process how to live God's Word.

Don't feel as if each lesson has to be finished in one sitting; take a few blocks of time throughout the week if you need to. The goal of this study is to dig deeply into Scripture and uncover how it applies to your life, to deeply engage the mind and the heart. Projects, stories, and Bible study all play a role in it. You may be drawing or journaling or interacting with sheltered or food insecure people in your community. At each group meeting you will discuss your experience in working through that week's lesson.

TERRIFIC RESOURCES FOR FURTHER PERSONAL STUDY

www.biblegateway.com

WHO IS JOSEPH, AND WHY DOES HE MATTER?

WHO WAS JOSEPH IN HISTORY?

:: Joseph was the eleventh son of Jacob (father of the twelve tribes of Israel) and his mother was Rachel.

:: From an early age, Joseph had dreams and revelations from God. He specifically dreamed that his brothers and parents would all bow down to him one day.

:: Joseph was hated by his ten older brothers, and they sold him into slavery.

:: Joseph served as a servant in the house of Potiphar.

:: Joseph was unjustly imprisoned when Potiphar's wife reported him for rape.

:: With God's revelation to Joseph through dreams, he went on to help Pharaoh lead Eygpt out of a great famine and was given tremendous authority, second only to Pharaoh himself.

WHO IS JOSEPH IN SCRIPTURE?

:: Joseph's story threads through Genesis 37–50.

:: Joseph serves as a prototype of Christ.

:: Joseph serves as the biggest link between the patriarchs of Israel (Abraham, Isaac, and Jacob) and Moses and the prophets.

WHO IS JOSEPH IN GOD'S PLAN?

:: Joseph reveals God's character.

:: His story shows how God provided for his people far in advance of their need. It's an inspiration and encouragement to our faith and prayers.

:: His story shows how God can work our disobedience as well as our obedience to accomplish his purposes.

:: The favor of God on Joseph's life displays what it means to be called by God for a specific purpose.

:: His life shows how God is sovereign over good and evil, blessing and famine.

HOW DOES JOSEPH'S LIFE ULTIMATELY POINT TO CHRIST?

:: Joseph's obedience through difficulty results in the preservation of the future nation of Israel and the line of Christ. This is both a means to Christ and a picture of Christ.

:: The events of Joseph's life foreshadow the role and ministry of Jesus.

:: The pictures of redemption, forgiveness, and reconciliation all foreshadow the work of Christ on our behalf despite our rebellion.

INTRODUCTION:RESTLESS 1

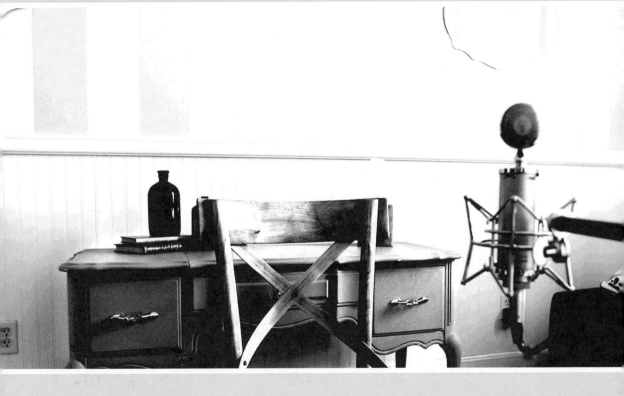

Pages 16–33 are intended for you to get acclimated
to this study on your own, after you watch the first
video. Flip to page 34 for Video Teaching.

Something in me is restless, and I know I'm not alone. I think we are all aching for some magical great noble purpose to squeeze into the holes of our ordinary lives.

We are numb.

We are bored.

And yet, every once in a while our hearts race just a little. Not like when we were kids and we heard the words *Disney World*. Not even as intensely as when we heard the ice-cream truck. But every once in a while they quicken.

Why such a restlessness for purpose?

Because it is possible to waste our lives.

These words haunt me and point to one of the greatest fears of mankind. We aren't sure we matter. We live *with* lots of things and lots of people, but do we live *for* something?

We all desperately want to live for something. We die a little inside when we think we aren't living for something, and are ready to die when we think we can't. But that purpose feels slippery sometimes. We glance over at people functioning in their gifts and God is using them in big ways, and we want that. But it can feel so far away.

There is a beautiful verse in the Bible hidden away in Acts, describing the end of David's life: "When David had served God's purpose in his own generation, he fell asleep" (13:36).

King David was a man after God's heart who lived a passionate mess of a life, but he sought after God and God's will. God used him to change the history of the world. This verse has two truths that make me tremble:

1. God has a unique purpose for each of us in our generation.

2. We have the choice to live that purpose or not.

I want to serve the purpose of God in my generation before I fall asleep.

I am calling you to the same. If we as a generation full of individuals serve the purposes of God on this earth, we could see our unwasted lives move together and change eternity.

I want to attempt something here together: to dream.

First, let's assume that if we are breathing, we have a specific purpose for being here. Every one of us with breath in our lungs still has something left to do.

I want to dream of what those purposes may be.

I wish I could promise magical moments with angels scripting visions in the sky just for you. I wish I could promise that at the end of this study, you would never feel empty, numb, or bored again. I can't.

But if you go here with me, the drum beat I hear in the distance, the one that makes my heart move faster—you will hear it. And maybe if we all hear and respond, we will see God move. We will know why we are here, why we are alive, what we are to do as a generation, and what we are to do as individuals.

So I am going to ask you to join me in a very uncomfortable process during this study. I want you to dare to believe that God has a vision for how you are to spend your life here. Because finding and accomplishing this vision is quite possibly the greatest responsibility we have as a generation, second only to knowing and loving God.

WE WERE DESIGNED TO DREAM

Genesis 1 tells of God creating the world and creating mankind.

Then God said, "Let us make mankind in our image, in our likeness, so that they may rule over . . . all the creatures that move along the ground" (verse 26).

So after several days of creating something out of nothing, God created people to reflect his glory, nature, and character on this earth. To lead, create, care, and love.

God blessed them and said to them, "Be fruitful and increase in number; fill the earth and subdue it" (verse 28).

God created man in his image for a purpose. In the beginning only two jobs were ascribed to man:

1. Fill the earth with image bearers.
2. Make the world better: take chaos and give it order.

When we were born, we were given certain resources. Now we are to take whatever we are given and use it to reflect God and to serve people during our short time on earth. That's why we were given abilities above animals—to create, build, serve, lead, envision, and get after it. We have the unique talent of being able to see a need, and then create a way to meet that need. In that way, we reflect God.

WE ARE CALLED TO DREAM

Through the prophet Joel, God said this of the future: "I will pour out my Spirit on all people. Your sons and daughters will prophesy, your old men will dream dreams, your young men will see visions" (Joel 2:28).

This day has happened. It's here.

The Holy Spirit flooded the earth at Pentecost. Immediately after, Peter reminded the apostles of the promise of that day: "No, this is what was spoken by the prophet Joel: 'In the last days, God says, I will pour out my Spirit on all people. Your sons and daughters will prophesy, your young men will see visions, your old men will dream dreams'" (Acts 2:16–17).

Why? So that "everyone who calls on the name of the Lord will be saved" (Acts 2:21).

You see, our creative God has an infinite number of creative plans to make himself known through us in unique and beautiful ways.

WE MUST DREAM

Dream. It seems a luxurious word, existing for the free and wealthy. It's a word my friend FeeFee tears up when she hears.

FeeFee lives in rural Haiti, in a tiny mortar house, with her three young children and a husband. Every day she builds a fire and pops popcorn to sell for five cents a bag outside their little home to help pay for her kids' schooling. Her husband, August, lays brick every day he can find work. She and her husband survive. But do they have the luxury of dreaming?

They lay bricks and pop popcorn, and sometimes when their children sit down for dinner FeeFee can only offer them leftover popcorn. But FeeFee tears up at the word *dream* because she lives closely attached to one. She dreams that her children would have a better life than she has—a life without popcorn meals.

If you are reading this book, you likely have the luxurious obligation to dream. We live at a time in history that affords us something that many have died for: the freedom and opportunity to dream and accomplish those dreams.

Most of us are not engaged in a home-turf war. We are not looking for food in trash cans. We are not slaves without rights. We are not simply surviving physically, as many, possibly even most generations before us have.

We possess the right, the power, and the resources to dream, and we take it for granted. We numb out and miss that we hold more resources than nearly any generation has before us. With our freedom, with our comfort, with our security, we get to dream. We get to build. We get to hope. We get to change. We get to influence. We get to respond.

It is a glorious luxury, and our greatest responsibility.

FOUR STARTING PLACES

We all come into this process from a different place, and all of us will need different things during it. This road will be unique to every single person. There are, however, a few different places that may describe just where you are. Can you see yourself in any of them?

COMFORTABLE

You don't know if you are living on purpose or not. You are busy, surviving, and somewhat content. Sometimes you may be bored, but in general your life is full, and you aren't one to overanalyze. Maybe you are beginning to wake up and hurt for more, but even that concept just made you nervous.

Questions you may be asking:

:: "Shouldn't I just feel thankful for what I have instead of wanting more?"

:: "What is wrong with being comfortable and happy?"

:: "Shouldn't I just be faithful where I am?"

To you, I would say this: "There is a time for everything . . . a time to search and a time to give up . . . a time to tear and a time to mend, a time to be silent and a time to speak," and on and on (Ecclesiastes 3:1, 6–7).

This may be your time to tear up and your time to search and speak and consider. For a short season I want you to consider that there may be more. Because I would rather you be unsettled for a minute and sure that you are in the will of God, than content in the wrong place.

THIRSTY

You hurt. Inside you are longing for more. You are begging for more purpose than you currently feel. But you don't know if your restless heart is your enemy—making you unsettled—or your friend—pushing you toward more. You are not satisfied, but you don't know what to do about it. You are asking yourself: "Is there more? And if there is, how do I find it?"

Questions you may be asking:

:: "Is it wrong to want more?"

:: "Does God have some secret purpose and I am just missing it?"

:: "What if there is no clear direction? What then?"

The apostle Paul wrote from prison, "I urge you to live a life worthy of the calling you have received" (Ephesians 4:1).

There remained a restlessness in Paul throughout his life. He urgently went about the work of God and asked us to do the same. I don't know if your restless heart is sinful or from God. But I do know that God often awakens and moves me toward more by using a deep discontentment and a unsettling feeling of dissatisfaction. Many times when I longed for more, sure enough, he had more for me. We will deal with all of these questions, so don't preach away that restlessness yet.

RUNNING FREE

Some of you are living it. You feel purpose. You are running full speed ahead in obedience, and you have watched God move around you. You know what you are made to do, and perhaps you are already doing it. You have already moved through a season of feeling numb or satisfied and have become thirsty and found more. Life is full and hard but rich and fulfilling too.

Questions you may be asking:

:: "Do I even need this? I already know the answer to a lot of these questions. Why should I do this study?"

Some of my most on-target friends have needed this study more than anyone else because we all forget.

Let us throw off everything that hinders and the sin that so easily entangles. And let us run with perseverance the race marked out for us, fixing our eyes on Jesus, the pioneer and perfecter of faith . . . so that you will not grow weary and lose heart.

HEBREWS 12:1–3

I have been in all of these places over and over again and you will too. We start running the race we were meant to run, and then we realize after mile five that we have accidentally signed up for a marathon. And before we know it, we are bored or restless all over again. Let this study hand you water on your run. Let this process fill you with new strength and focus, and remind you afresh of your calling so that you will keep running and not grow weary. We are not home yet, and I pray this time will help you persevere in your race.

AT THE STARTING LINE

Or maybe you've realized that you don't really know God, that you don't actually have a personal relationship with him, where you talk every day and you look to him and live for him. If that's the case, then before you go any further, read the "How to Find God" page in the back of this book. It'll be the best, most important thing you'll ever do.

RESPOND

Take a minute alone and pray before you move ahead. Then take a few minutes before God and write out your answers to the questions below. After you are done, come back together in your small group and discuss.

Which of the stages described above do you most relate to right now?

When was the last time you dreamt about doing something specific in your life?

Are you coming into this study with any hurt and disappointment regarding your dreams? If so, describe it.

When you were a kid, what did you think you would be when you grew up? Why did you want to be that?

What stops you from running full steam ahead? From dreaming? From obeying? Respond to these questions in relation to each category below.

Physical (examples: time, energy, finances, responsibilities, health)

Emotional (examples: depression, fear, insecurity)

Relational (examples: tension, hurt from childhood, discouragement)

Spiritual (examples: belief, motives, strongholds, sin, shame)

When you anticipate having the freedom to dream, what are you afraid of that keeps you from doing it right now?

Do you feel discontent right now? If so, how does that discontentment tie into a desire for purpose?

In light of all of this, what do you most hope to get out of this time?

THE LIFE OF JOSEPH

Every one of us has been given a unique story and unique resources, people, and gifts. We have each been put in specific places in which we are to build the continuing story of God. Apart from the person of Christ in Scripture, no one else demonstrates that like Joseph. So we will follow the journey of a man who was chosen by God for a specific task, but who felt like he was wandering for most of his life. But all the while, God was turning Joseph into a man who could ultimately fulfill God's purposes.

There were some things that Joseph understood about this, and there were more that he didn't. But he ran headfirst into the story that God had prepared for him. His life was used to create, build, and serve purposes that would last forever. Faith marked Joseph's imperfect life, and while he faced mundane days and days that were unthinkably tragic, he completed the work that God had for him before he died.

I want that. There is joy in being in the will of God, and used by him for great purposes. There is peace there, even when God's will feels mundane or difficult. So we will watch this man live faith in front of us. And while we watch, we will look at our own lives.

OUR THREADS

Just as we see the threads of God's purpose weaving through Joseph's life, our goal here is to lay out the threads already running through our own lives. When we see how they begin to weave together, we better understand ourselves. We're freer to dream intentionally about how to use our lives to bring God glory.

WHAT IS THIS STUDY ALL ABOUT?

This process will help you uncover the unique ways you have been built, the stories that have been given to you, the passions in your soul, the people in your path, the places you are to be, and the purposes the Holy Spirit is calling you toward.

This study is a chance to lay out what you have—what you know—and offer it to God. I should mention that we have no way of knowing what he will say to do with all this, but we begin by laying it out and handing it over.

WHY DOES IT MATTER?

Without some effort, we will waste our minutes, our days . . . our lives. So putting thought into spending our time and resources for the glory of God may be the most important thing we can do.

Think of it this way:

God's story + my materials + need + the Holy Spirit = my purpose

Or, to be more specific,

The story of God through Scripture

+

An understanding of myself and my resources

+

Taking inventory of the need around me

+

The mystery of following the Holy Spirit's leading

=

Obediently living my purpose

Your threads will serve as a:

:: catalyst to move you to action;

:: filter for opportunities as they present themselves;

:: compass to direct you toward God's purposes for you.

As you begin this journey consider the three things holding you back from dreaming. (For example, need for approval, lack of resources, fear.)

Take some time alone this week, laying down each of these fears and barriers and asking God to reveal visions of how your life may be used for his purposes in these weeks together.

SEE ::

Watch video session one: INTRODUCTION: RESTLESS

Use streaming instructions on inside cover or DVD.

Take notes if you like.

A S K ::

Use session one: RESTLESSS

Conversation Cards for group discussion.

GOD'S STORY :: 2

Work through pages 40–59 on your own before your next group meeting and before you watch the next video teaching.

My son Cooper was born and lived three and a half years of his life in Africa. He is five now and is wrestling with the fact that his skin color is a few—strike that—*many* shades darker than the rest of his family's. He keeps running his hand up and down my arm and asking me, "Where can we go, so I can get skin like this?"

He's not speaking with knowledge of the painful history of his skin color in our country yet. Right now he just wants to be like his family. His identity is unique in our family. He has a heritage that each of us appreciates deeply, but we do not share it. So he quietly asks me as we lay in bed before prayers:

"Why did God make me born in Africa?"

"Why did God put me in another mommy's tummy?"

"Why did God make me?"

I can't deny that the answers to many of my son's questions are painful. Abandonment usually undergirds the beautiful tragedy of adoption. Even though he finds himself in a loving family now, we can never make that painful truth go away.

It's usually dark as we lay in bed to pray and talk. Cooper doesn't know that every time he asks me these questions, I have tears running down my face as I preach my guts out in his bottom bunk:

"Not one part of you is by accident, Cooper. God made you and placed you in your African mama's tummy. He knew even then that I would be your forever mama and we would be your forever family. We were made for you and you were made for us.

"Cooper, you were made to show the world God. Everything that God gives you, your Africa, your America, your dark skin and your strong legs, your hurts, your words, your blessings, your smart mind . . . everything you have is to use for God while you are here.

"And God will show you how. Soon we will be in heaven with God forever, but while we are here now, we have to use all we have for God."

My five-year-old needs to know his life was on purpose and for a purpose. He wants to know he wasn't an accident. I can't take away the pain of his story, but I can tell him there is purpose. We all want to know we are not accidents. We all want to know our stories are going somewhere on purpose.

Something deep down inside us is made to live for a story bigger than ourselves—the story of the one who made us. Any other version of this story will consistently feel shallow and empty.

He has also set eternity in the hearts of men.

ECCLESIASTES 3:11 NIV 1984

Cooper will never make sense of his life until he understands that eternal story, and the God who made him and placed him in his spot. It's a big earth, and when Cooper studies it, he sees countries separated by a huge ocean and he feels lost and small in it.

I think a lot of us feel lost and small.

And because of that we desperately want to find "God's will for me." We want to know that we exist on purpose and for a purpose. We often try to find "God's will for me" without simply first understanding God's will. But we will only ever discover his will for us within God's will for this earth, for eternity, and for his people. We were made for this story—his story. And yes, he wrote little parts for each of us in his story. Or else we wouldn't exist.

STUDY ::

Read Hebrews 10:36–12:3

RESPOND

In your own words summarize the story of God's work on earth as told in Hebrews 10:36–12:3.

What was the most defining thing about these men and women?

Define faith. (Hebrews 11:1)

In what different ways did the people in those verses live out their faith?

Describe the actions of someone without faith. (Hebrews 10:38–39)

Describe some of the things that happen because of faith in these lives. (Hebrews 11)

The author of Hebrews has a goal for the readers. He wants them to understand the history of God on earth for a reason. What is his goal in sharing this history of faith? (Hebrews 12:1–3)

What do you think was the main thing God was accomplishing on earth through these generations of people?

WHAT IS GOD AFTER?

My little Cooper, Rahab, Oprah, Abraham Lincoln, Alexander the Great, and every other single human on the face of the earth has found his or her story in the confines of God's story. The history of the world fits in a small crevice of the history of God. And throughout that history, God is after one great purpose. And every one of our unique callings will fit into this one.

God is most after his glory.

Glory is the visible expression of God's character on this earth.

So just as Abraham in faith followed God into the wilderness, bringing God glory, when you bravely obey or sacrifice or risk in faith to follow God, you bring him glory.

God's chief pursuit is that his glory, through us, would fill the earth. Everyone of our unique callings will display hints of the glory of our God.

THE PROBLEM

We ache to be a part of something great, and it makes us nervous at the same time. We were built for this, but we all fight hundreds of mixed motives and fears.

Jesus said of us, "Whoever believes in me . . . they will do even greater things than these" (John 14:12). It almost sounds blasphemous to do even greater things than Jesus. We rarely say it, but often when we start to have great thoughts or visions, we quickly dismiss them, afraid that we may become arrogant or prideful. Or much worse, simply that we would *appear* prideful.

* * *

God gave man two commands: be fruitful and fill the earth. He kept repeating this phrase in history in a beautiful effort to fill the earth with his image through us—an earth full of the glory of God.

Instead of filling the earth with God's glory, humans they came together to build a tower and to make a name for themselves (Genesis 11). John Piper says of this tower and of our souls, "Man was made to rely on God and give him glory. Instead man chose to rely on himself and seek his own glory—to make a name for himself."[1]

We all will have to fight this. Perhaps it is the biggest hurdle we must cross to living our purposes. At the base of our souls, are we building for God or us?

Take just a minute and pray. Ask God to reveal your motives.

What is the driving force of your life?

---

1. John Piper, "God Created Us for His Glory," Desiring God (blog), July 27, 1980. www.desiringgod.org/resource-library/sermons/god-created-us-for-his-glory.

Whatever you just wrote, within this great story, God provided the remedy to our souls. To overcome us, God would make a great sacrifice.

> [Christ] is the radiance of the glory of God and the exact imprint of his nature, and he upholds the universe by the word of his power. After making purification for sins, he sat down at the right hand of the Majesty on high.
>
> **HEBREWS 1:3** ESV

Christ in us would be the hope of glory (Colossians 1:27). For the joy set before him, he endured the cross. It is a joy that we share. The joy of a forever with a God who is entirely good and who chose us to become his children. The whole earth will be full of his glory; evil will be crushed. Until then we run, showing God to the world and not growing weary.

This history of faith we read about in Hebrews is there because God wants us to see we have a part in his story. He wants us to live motivated by faith in the unseen, and to run.

So we fight the desire to build our own towers. When we do the great things he prepared in advance for us to do (Ephesians 2:10), but we do them in and through and for the name and glory of God.

GREATER THINGS

We were made to do great things, but we cannot live with motives unchecked. If our motives are the glory of God, we have tremendous freedom to dream with hearts that are completely his.

I want to have a faith that God can move through.

I want Cooper to understand he isn't just made for a purpose; he was placed in this time and space for the greatest imaginable purpose. He will show God to a world that doesn't know him, in his beautiful and unique way. He will bring light to darkness. He will assemble the pieces of his life not into a tower for his name that would only crumble, but he will assemble them for the name and glory of the one God Almighty.

Well, he's five, and currently we are working on not throwing rocks, but that's the hope. That's the prayer. That's the sermon he's going to keep hearing.

Our hearts must be completely his before we can start to dream.

For the eyes of the LORD move to and fro throughout the earth that He may strongly support those whose heart is completely His.

2 CHRONICLES 16:9 NASB

WHO ARE YOU, LORD? & WHAT DO YOU WANT FOR ME?

Read John 17:1-16. In light of what you read, answer the questions above.

REFLECT

> [Christ] is the radiance of the glory of God and the exact imprint of
> his nature . . .
>
> **HEBREWS 1:3** ESV

If Christ is the exact imprint of God's nature, use the chart below and on the next page
to describe how Christ reacted to each thing listed, using your knowledge of Christ's
story and the Bible verses you just read for guidance. In the far-right column, write a few
descriptive words about what those actions tell us about God's nature.

	CHRIST'S ACTION TOWARD . . .	GOD'S NATURE
Temptation	he fought it and was victorious over it (see Mark 1:13)	persevering, holy
Religiousness		
Sinners		

Sickness		
Forgiveness		
The devil		
This life		
Heaven		
Money		

IMAGINE

Draw an image of the glory of God. This is an impossibly abstract assignment. But I think sometimes we never analyze abstract concepts like glory. What does it remind you of? What image comes to mind? What would it look like if we all displayed God's glory here? Use your imagination.

For the earth will be filled with the knowledge of the glory of the LORD as the waters cover the sea.

HABAKKUK 2:14

DEAL

> [God] will bring to light what is hidden in darkness and will expose the motives of the heart. At that time each will receive their praise from God.
>
> **1 CORINTHIANS 4:5**

What are some of the mixed motives you need to deal with?

Have your motives ever stopped you from doing something you wanted to do for God? If so, what were those dreams?

Has your fear of *appearing* arrogant every held you back? If so describe it.

We have a lot of freedom to dream, but there is not freedom in our motives. The hidden parts of us are the very most important to God. Two people can accomplish the same thing with different motives and one will please God and one won't. If you realize that you are doing a good thing for a not-so-good purpose, don't despair. Dedicate it to God right now and ask him to commandeer it for his glory.

CONSIDER

> Faith is confidence in what we hope for and assurance about what we do not see.
>
> **HEBREWS 11:1**

How confident are you that the story of God is real? Explain your answer, and how it affects your life.

How confident are you that Jesus is your savior? Explain your answer, and how that confidence or absence of it affects your life.

How confident are you that God has specific purposes for you in his story? Explain. What difference has that made to you?

Talk about it.

I'll be honest. I have given my life to God's story, and there are still days I wonder if it is all real. It's okay if you waver sometimes. God holds us in place with him; we don't hold ourselves. Where your faith is weak, pray and ask him for more. "I do believe; help me overcome my unbelief!" (Mark 9:24).

CONCLUSION

> I have brought you glory on earth by finishing the work you gave me to do.
>
> **JOHN 17:4**

Jesus said this before he died.

I want to say that before I die too.

I recently lay in my hotel room listening as Larry King interviewed Daniel Radcliffe about the final Harry Potter movie. Daniel said a beautiful thing about his role in these epic films. "I always knew that anyone who was given this role would have the same fame. It was never about me. It was about this franchise. I was simply a part of something bigger."[2]

I teared up when I heard it. I had spent the day meeting and greeting important people in the book world, in some small ways trying to become important.

---

2. *Larry King Live*, July 10, 2011, CNN.

And after a day of trying to become important, my heart broke as I realized I was only a small part of an epic story—the very most successful franchise that ever was. And anyone could play my part. I was reading lines of a story written before creation, and I was but a breath, playing my tiny part in it. It would never be me that was important. I would simply play the part that was given to me.

Isaiah 40 describes the enormity of a God who sits above the circle of the earth; its inhabitants are like grass to him. "All people are like grass, and all their faithfulness is like the flowers of the field" (v. 6). It is not that we are insignificant. Rather, he is so significant that comparatively, we are but a breath.

He breathes in and out, and a generation has already passed away.

I have lived a lot of my life on the back row fearing that if I dream or live great dreams I may steal glory from God. Who am I to even think such a thing? As my friend Christine Caine says, "Who am I to dare think, that on my very best day, I could ever take one little piece of the glory of God?"

So instead of fearing or craving greatness, crave God and run your guts out.

NOTES

The arrow below represents God's story, beginning with the Trinity and creation, and ending (at least from your viewpoint) when you meet him in heaven. Based on the scriptures we've studied and your own experience of the Bible, fill in more key points on the time line of the story of God. Or fill it with notes from the video talk.

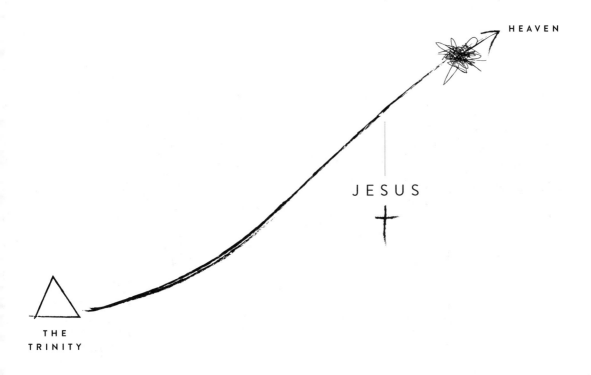

HEAVEN

JESUS

THE
TRINITY

SEE ::

Watch video session two: GOD'S STORY

Use streaming instructions on inside cover or DVD.

Take notes if you like.

ASK ::

Use session two: GOD'S STORY

Conversation Cards for group discussion.

GIFTS :: 3

Work through pages 66–83 on your own before your next group meeting and before you watch the next video teaching.

Jessica and Hannah pulled their chairs together during our study in Austin. Jessica gripped in her hands the scribbles revealing her most sacred moments. As she looked back over the list of times when she had felt God's pleasure and felt fully satisfied in her life, they all had something to do with a stage—performing in a school musical, being elected student-council president, a talk she'd given at a leadership summit.

She realized she was about to have to share them with Hannah, whom she barely knew. So she cynically laughed and said, "I am not sure if these moments display my gifts or my selfishness."

I have watched Jessica wrestle internally for clarity of purpose for years. Yet when that girl prays or teaches, the whole room worships. She exudes an authentic passion. And yet Jessica is terrified of herself. She is gifted—a leader, a teacher, a visionary—but she is only barely using her gifts because of many distinct fears. As we sat together digging up all her fears, she boiled it down for me.

She is afraid if she runs too fast with her strengths as a single woman, that men will find her too strong—too abrasive. She is afraid of dreaming and trying, and then having to face failure or disappointment. She is afraid of her own selfish ambition or the sin that may come out if she really pursued opportunities to use her gifting. She wonders if God made a mistake. Why would he give a woman all this strength?

That night Hannah looked at her and said, "These moments that you feel so happy—performing and leading—those would be my worst nightmares. Your pleasure in those moments, God has put that in you."

Jessica called me later to say, "For some reason I thought everyone craved a stage. Maybe I have a responsibility to quit being afraid of my motives and start using the gifts and passions God has put in me."

Jessica is superanalytical, and so am I, and so are a lot of you. We often overanalyze clear, simple truths. We tell ourselves it is right to be afraid. I don't know what your fears are, but I know if they aren't from God they are from the enemy, and they need to be taken apart.

Moving into our God-given purposes requires an understanding of our God-given gifts and strengths.

Before we learned to be afraid and insecure and full of mixed motives we were children, with pure, simple gifts and abilities. Every one of us. Sparks of our future can be seen in our childhood. Our simple childhood fantasies contain a lot of information about the way God built us to live out his purposes.

God revealed a spark, a hint of his purpose for Joseph and in what we will study today. But the road to living that purpose would be long.

S T U D Y ::

Read Genesis 37:1–11

What was God revealing to Joseph in these dreams?

About Joseph?

About his plan?

Describe Joseph's actions following his dreams.

What was the result of Joseph's actions?

READ 1 CORINTHIANS 12

Who gives the gifts in these verses?

Who has a gift?

What are the gifts' purpose?

What do you read about our unique individual purposes?

How do our unique roles make up one body?

Describe some of the tensions that occur when many unique pieces are challenged to work together as one body for one purpose.

What happens if we each play our part?

BUILT TO RUN

In the past month, somehow I have ended up with my kids in two different settings driving go-carts. The first track was at GattiTown; it was a circle the size of a small swimming pool. The cars didn't go anywhere. They just bumped into each other in this little, contained, suffocating circle of a track. It wasn't a track—it was a parking lot. It cost about one dollar to ride, and after my kids finished, they hopped off and ran to the next thing. They didn't even look back.

Then one night while Zac was traveling I needed to get my little people out, so I researched go-carts and found a new track just outside of town.

I threw everyone in the car and we drove to this huge warehouse. We walked in, and they issued us helmets and wanted to know if we had any heart conditions. *Ummm . . . where the heck are we?* Then the man behind the register reported that the final tally of our crew's adventure would add up to over a hundred dollars. We had driven all this way. Thankfully my two youngest were too short for what was about to happen anyway.

To prevent utter devastation, I painfully paid for only my eleven- and thirteen–year-olds' passes. The two little ones and I took our seats in the bleachers to watch the most incredible race play out. They were strapped in, and hit their pedals and chased each other at ungodly speeds around more than a mile of track. They were completely free and brave and racing, and I could barely breathe watching them.

It was the most epic go-cart track I'd ever seen.

They did bump into each other occasionally and into the side rails too, but for the most part they just raced their guts out, staying on track and having the time of their lives. They'll never forget that race.

I think most of us have paid a dollar and found ourselves in some stagnant rubber car bumping into each other.

But what if . . .

What if the things you love to do actually converge with God's will?

What if you had God-given gifts and he wanted to turn you loose using them?

What if you were built for a track and you are camped out in a parking lot?

I have talked to so many people who are driving around a parking lot, and they can't figure out why they feel so discontent. They are afraid that if they pull out of the lot and onto a real track:

They wouldn't actually have anything to contribute.

They would go too fast—get out of control.

They would lose.

They would wreck.

People would judge them.

In the passage we just studied together, Joseph hoped his gifts were for his own glory. I picture this as a parking-lot season for him. He was brash and arrogant and using his God-given gift, but for his own purposes. He was crashing into his brothers with it. But in these cases, there is a purpose for all of this; there is a track with side rails; there is a reason God gives us gifts. We will experience the pleasure of racing while God is using us, but our gifts' primary purpose is for building up others.

Let's look at the verses that come immediately after this awesome vision of purpose in 1 Corinthians 12.

WHO ARE YOU, LORD? & WHAT DO YOU WANT FOR ME?

Read 1 Corinthians 13:1-12. In light of what you read, answer the questions above.

GIFTS AND ABILITIES

Every one of us has natural abilities and Spirit-given gifts.

As we study the life of Joseph, we will learn that he is an excellent leader, good with people, and great with business and strategy. These were strengths imbedded in his personality and cultivated through his years of leading within Potiphar's home and then in prison. Whether or not he believed in God, these were his strengths as a man.

> Every good and perfect gift is from above, coming down from the Father of the heavenly lights.
>
> **JAMES 1:17**

God had also equipped Joseph with a spiritual, supernatural gift to interpret dreams. This gift was testament to the existence and power of Joseph's God and could not be easily explained without faith in the supernatural. God would go on to develop and use both Joseph's spiritual and natural gifts for the welfare of others and the glory of himself.

I was saved and filled with the Spirit at seventeen years old, but as a child I did have strengths in leadership and strategy that were clear to my family and at times to me. But when I was filled with God's Spirit at the moment I trusted in Christ for salvation, God took my natural abilities to gather younger girls, and I began to teach my Bible. I taught—strike that—I *preached*. I had a new supernatural gift of teaching. I had never seen it before, and it just poured out of me.

So now my natural abilities were being used supernaturally for God's purposes, and the Spirit was giving me a new gift that I could use to show his glory more fully on this earth.

Let me be clear. I can only see this now because I'm in my mid-thirties looking back on that time. When I was first experiencing it, I was uncertain and insecure, and had no idea what the words *spiritual gifts* even meant. And I can promise you my gifts were wild and undeveloped. I was seventeen, for crying out loud. This is a lifelong journey of discovering and growing in our giftings. Maybe you have seen hints of your gifts, maybe it is perfectly clear to you, or maybe you think you have nothing good to offer.

God is not holding out on you. While I can look back and see the sparks of God growing and revealing my gifts and abilities, for most of the last decade I have been focused on changing diapers and cooking chicken rather than growing in my gifts. Legitimate fears and insecurities also held me back. So as we begin the process of discovery here, I just want to take the pressure off. I don't know what is around the corner for you, and I possess no magic formula to twist God's arm and have him tell you. We are just going to dig a little. We are going to get under the hood and see what is in you—what God has given you to bring him glory. With God's

Word, prayer, space to think, and community, let's see what happens

REFLECT

First, use the chart below to identify a highlight from each life stage when you felt pleasure in what you were doing. When was a moment you remember being proud and satisfied? Do not overthink it. Just write down the first things that come to mind.

Once you've filled in the highlight column, go back and fill in the next column with a couple descriptive words to answer the question, "What specifically about these moments was satisfying to you?"

Here are some questions to get you thinking:

What were you great at?

What did you love to do?

What surprised you?

Whom did you love, and why did you love them?

What did you learn about yourself?

What did you dream about?

	HIGHLIGHT	SATISFACTION
example	painting with my grandfather	using art to communicate
0–6		
7–12		
13–18		
19–24		
25+		

INVENTORY

Below is a short list of some examples of gifts mentioned throughout Scripture. These are just to get you thinking. Some might jump right out at you and say, "This is you!" Others you might not be sure of. If you would like to delve into spiritual gifts further, see what exactly each word means, and even help discover which ones seem to fit you, there are plenty of resources and Bible commentaries that can take you down that road. Here are a couple:

:: *Strengths Finder 2.0* (book) by Tom Rath (Gallup Press, 2007). You can also access the corresponding online test at *https://www.gallupstrengthscenter.com*. It's a small cost, but has been a helpful tool for many.

:: LifeWay Spiritual Gifts Survey (online test), *http://www.lifeway.com/lwc/files/lwcF_MYCS_030526_Spiritual_Gifts_Survey.pdf.*

:: SpiritualGiftsTest.com (online test).

In addition to 1 Corinthians 12, these are other great passages for further study of gifts:

:: Romans 12

:: Ephesians 4

:: 1 Peter 4

Once you've had some time to think about it, circle below the gifts that you have seen God use in your life in the past.

Prophecy // Teaching // Exhortation // Encouragement // Service // Giving // Leadership // Mercy // Apostleship // Wisdom // Knowledge // Faith // Miracles // Healing // Administration // Discernment // Evangelism // Pastoring // Shepherding // Teaching // Hospitality // Missions

Describe two or three times you remember God using these gifts through you.

REMEMBER

We can't really have a good perspective on ourselves. With the two projects above in hand, sit down with a friend or roommate or family member and discuss these questions and your memories. You can do this over the phone or over coffee. Here are some questions to ask.

When have you seen me operating in my sweet spot?

What do you think I do well?

In what ways have you seen me grow and develop my gifts in the last few years?

Have I helped you grow? If so, how?

As you look through Project 1, what stands out to you?

REFLECT

Turn to Project 1 of this chapter, look back at your five life highlights, and choose one word about why each moment was satisfying to you. Chart each moment and word as a point on the arrow below. We will be using this arrow again as we move forward.

Now, reflecting on all of the projects, scriptures, and what you learned from family and friends so far, begin to narrow down five strengths most evident in your life. These can be spiritual gifts or natural abilities. You will have a bunch, no doubt, but try to narrow down to your top five.

1. _____

2. _____

3. _____

4. _____

5. _____

CONCLUSION

Eric Liddell was born in 1902, the son of missionaries in China. His story is retold in the epic film *Chariots of Fire*. Eric felt called to give his life to God, and in that pursuit he trained and planned to become a missionary, like his parents. But Eric had a gift. He could run, and every door was opening for him to do it. Doors opened all the way to the Olympics. As the film portrays Eric processing his calling and his gifts with his sister, he says these famous words: "I believe God made me for a purpose, but he also made me fast. And when I run I feel his pleasure."[3]

Some of us are hung up on looking for superspiritual gifts. But what if you are just fast? What if you are a great musician? What if you excel at accounting? What if you feel God's pleasure as you design buildings or format PTA calendars?

When do you feel God's pleasure?

Something about the answer to this question determines the unique things he has given you to use while you are here. There is no spiritual and secular divide. We have built these divisions. "Whatever you do, do it all for the glory of God" (1 Corinthians 10:31). Even the seemingly small and the boring parts.

We are simply gathering materials during this process. These raw materials of our lives could come together and be used to play our part in blessing others and building God's kingdom.

---

3. Hugh Hudson, director, *Chariots of Fire* (Enigma Productions, 1981).

SEE ::

Watch video session three: GIFTS

Use streaming instructions on inside cover or DVD.

Take notes if you like.

ASK ::

Use session three: GIFTS

Conversation Cards for group discussion.

SUFFERING :: 4

Work through pages 90–106 on your own before your next group meeting and before you watch the next video teaching.

I live in Austin, Texas, not Africa. And yet anyone who lives in Austin is very familiar with the word *gazelle*.

Gilbert Tuhabonye grew up in Burundi. Similar to my son's neighboring Rwanda, it is a country familiar with tribal war. Gilbert was given a gift like Eric Liddell's; he was fast. He ran to get water. He ran five miles to and from school. He ran to feed his family's cows. In school, Gilbert began to run competitively, with realistic aspirations of running in the Olympics.

But on October 21, 1993, a tribal war was reawakened between the Hutus and Tutsis. Gilbert and more than a hundred of his Tutsi classmates were forced into a classroom and beaten and burnt to death. Nine hours later, Gilbert would miraculously crawl out from under his friends' charred bodies, badly burned himself, and run through the night to a future that no one could have imagined—except a creative and redeeming God. To give you a hint, it involves Austin and gazelles.

I know some of you reading this have not tasted suffering like Gilbert's, but I also know that every one of you has tasted some version of suffering. We live in a broken world, and it's just overflowing with it. As I write, my best friend is recovering from massive strokes as her husband is wrapping up their divorce. It's too painful to process. And I know that many of you can say the same.

We are all tempted to shut down when the fire gets too hot. But who would not lay under his friends' bodies and wish to die? Who would be brave enough to dig out and run? That's crazy, and yet that same passion is in us. Some of us have never dug out and seen there is something to run for.

This week will be a beautiful, painful journey. But the greatest thing you have to give to the world could be hidden in your darkest moments. What if your scars point to a greater story?

STUDY ::

Read Genesis 37:12–36
and Genesis 39

Jot down anything that jumps out to you as you read and study.

RESPOND

Chart Joseph's sufferings in these chapters on this arrow.

Joseph dreams
great dreams.

Brothers
betray him.

Describe Joseph's attitude through these years of suffering.

Was God in control of the favor in Joseph's life?

Was God in control of the suffering in Joseph's life?

Recount the ways God shows his presence in these years of suffering.

When given the opportunity to turn his back on God and to escape his circumstances, how did Joseph respond?

People who crossed Joseph's path in these trials saw the Lord's favor on him in the midst of terrible circumstances. What characteristics might Joseph have displayed that allowed people to see God in him?

PAINFUL SONGS

> Here is the world. Beautiful and terrible things will happen.
> Don't be afraid.
>
> **FREDERICK BUECHNER** [1]

On a Sunday right before my friend Sarah's stroke, drowning in the divorce that she had fasted and prayed would not happen, she and I sat together in church. Even though we weren't looking at each other, I could feel her crying and she could feel me crying. But we sang. Hands raised. Tears falling. We sang these words together.

> Bless the Lord O my soul,
> Whatever may pass and whatever lies before me
> Let me be singing when the evening comes. [2]

Sarah is still singing. Her voice isn't working yet and may never again, but her eyes sing with a peace that none of us understands. And her story is singing as thousands of people are following her recovery and watching as her soul blesses the Lord with no voice and a body that isn't working.

---

1. Frederick Buechner, *Wishful Thinking* (New York, HarperOne, 1993), 34.
2. Matt Redman, "10,000 Reasons," *10,000 Reasons* (Sparrow Records: 2011).

As another friend familiar with suffering says, "You have to thank God for the seemingly good and the seemingly bad, because really, we don't know the difference."

God has a will, and we cannot see all of it yet. God gives and he takes away. We have Scripture and we know his story in part, but what we won't fully know until we see him face-to-face is how our stories were working together for good within his story.

Joseph was either a slave or in prison for twenty years because of his brothers. Twenty years. It seems too long to be in the dark—long enough to grow bitter and run from God. But Joseph kept hoping and kept clinging to a sovereign God who could release him at any point.

WHY GOD MAY LET US SUFFER

1. JESUS IS BEST KNOWN THROUGH SUFFERING.

Every time I want to be mad at God because of suffering, he shows me Jesus.

I want to know Christ—yes, to know the power of his resurrection and participation in his sufferings.

PHILIPPIANS 3:10

And it is true. I have known Jesus most deeply in suffering; he seems to inhabit suffering, and he endured it first. He is not a God unfamiliar with suffering and he is near the brokenhearted. He is near our broken hearts.

2. WE GET STRONGER.

With suffering comes a morbid but helpful perspective that life is moving fast and earth is not our home. I used to live afraid my life wasn't going to work out just right. The more I surrender to suffering and joy and whatever God has for me, the more my fear becomes that I won't spend my life well. I can run farther and longer than I could before. I am not despairing; faith is growing.

Consider it pure joy, my brothers and sisters, whenever you face trials of many kinds, because you know that the testing of your faith produces perseverance. Let perseverance finish its work so that you may be mature and complete, not lacking anything.

JAMES 1:2-4

3. WE HURT FOR HEAVEN.

Sometimes the suffering around me is too much to bear, and I look around and think, *Done and done. Come Jesus.* We hurt because we don't belong here. But there is hope:

> Dear friends, do not be surprised at the fiery ordeal that has come on you to test you, as though something strange were happening to you. But rejoice inasmuch as you participate in the sufferings of Christ, so that you may be overjoyed when his glory is revealed.
>
> **1 PETER 4:12–13**

His glory will be revealed, and those who have suffered most will be the most overjoyed. But since we aren't home yet, there is much we can do in the meantime.

4. OUR LIVES COULD LEAVE A MARK.

Our lives are a breath, so if we are here for just a minute, I'd like my one little breath to feel more like a mighty gust of wind. And that takes surrender. It takes perseverance and not wasting my minutes away on Facebook or on complaining. The apostles walked away from painful persecution, "rejoicing because they had been counted worthy of suffering" (Acts 5:41).

Hear me. Even though it may seem counterintuitive, it is an honor to suffer. It is a privilege. And we are not to waste it. God wrote suffering into our stories and wants to redeem it for his glory. If we stop shaking our fists at him, we could possibly sit down and see we are running from a life in flames toward a great purpose—one that could never exist without the flames.

Joseph was a brat with a vision. And God was preparing him for that purpose. Joseph would save and lead nations, but first he had to learn who this story was about.

When Joseph first had a vision, he thought that vision was for his own glory. When that vision finally came true and his brothers were bowing before him, Joseph said these words:

You intended to harm me, but God intended it for good to accomplish what is now being done, the saving of many lives.

GENESIS 50:20

What if the very darkest moments of your life God intended for good, for the saving of lives?

2 CORINTHIANS 1:3-7

Praise be to the God and Father of our Lord Jesus Christ, the Father of compassion and the God of all comfort, who comforts us in all our troubles, so that we can comfort those in any trouble with the comfort we ourselves receive from God. For just as we share abundantly in the sufferings of Christ, so also our comfort abounds through Christ. If we are distressed, it is for your comfort and salvation; if we are comforted, it is for your comfort, which produces in you patient endurance of the same sufferings we suffer. And our hope for you is firm, because we know that just as you share in our sufferings, so also you share in our comfort.

STUDY

WHO ARE YOU, LORD? & WHAT DO YOU WANT FOR ME?

Read 2 Corinthians 1:3-7. In light of what you read, answer the questions above.

REFLECT

In the chart below, identify a memory from each life stage when you remember suffering. Do not overthink it. Just write down the first things that come to mind in the "Memory" column.

Here are some questions to get you thinking. (Some of you will have no problem remembering the most painful moments of your life. I am so sorry.)

Did anyone hurt you?

What circumstances were out of your control?

When did you feel afraid?

When do you remember crying?

Next, go back and write a couple of descriptive words to answer the question, "What specifically about that moment was most hurtful to you?"

	MEMORY	WHAT HURT
example	my parents divorced	insecure about future
0–7		
7–12		
13–18		
19–24		
25+		

CONSIDER

It is difficult for us to consider God's purposes for our suffering if we are still walking around with gaping, open wounds. Are they scars yet? Or still bleeding? When you look back at these moments, is there still a lot of pain in remembering? I am a big believer in Christian counseling, and that may be an important step in your healing, but no study or book or counselor can do what Jesus can do. He suffered and wants to walk with you through your suffering as the open wounds heal into scars, leaving a memory and a mark but losing their sting.

As you process your dark moments, write a letter to Jesus. If you are angry or sad, that is okay. Be honest and tell him your thoughts on these moments.

_____

_____

_____

_____

_____

_____

_____

_____

_____

_____

_____

_____

_____

_____

_____

PROJECT :: 2

REFLECT

I want to be sensitive to your processing. This project may not be appropriate yet. If you just wrote down things you have never shared with anyone or if you are still deeply grieving a loss or abuse, this project may be too difficult right now. So I am giving you permission to lay this project down for months or years, and take steps to seek healing from God, with the help you need from others.

If you are ready to move forward, devote some time to figuring out how you can best interact with these questions. Some of you are verbal processors, and others are internal processors. You can go through this project by yourself or with family or a friend.

Below, rewrite a list of each moment that you shared in Project 1. Then write beside it how that moment has played a part in shaping you.

Write some possible ways God could use each experience to help someone else.

REFLECT

Turn to Projects 1 and 3 in this chapter, look back at your five dark moments throughout your life again, choose one word to represent that event, and chart each moment on the arrow below.

We will continue to work with this arrow as we move forward.

Now, reflecting on all of the projects, scriptures, and what you learned from family and friends, begin to narrow down three to five passions that have been born from these dark places.

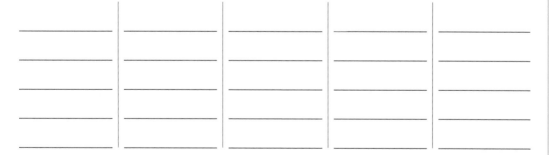

We often long to give to the world what we failed to receive growing up.

CONCLUSION

Gilbert from Burundi is still running; I see him run, because he lives in my neighborhood with his two daughters and his wife, Triphine. Gilbert was given the opportunity to train for the Olympics in the US and awarded a scholarship to Abilene Christian University. He built Gilbert's Gazelles into one of the most respected running training groups in the US, and he cofounded the Gazelle Foundation, whose mission is to build water projects in Burundi. He travels and speaks, sharing his scars so that he can share God's story.

As a young boy in Burundi he learned a saying: "It is easy to light a fire and difficult to extinguish it." He writes in his memoir, "I understand that saying much better now than I did. Though some would have liked to see me destroyed by flames, no one can extinguish the fire inside of me. The light God placed there still burns brightly." Then he writes, "I must go run now."[3]

What men meant for evil, God meant for good, for the saving of many lives. Fires are lit in our lives and they can burn to shine light or cause destruction; we get to decide which purpose they will serve.

---

3. Gilbert Tuhabonye and Gary Brozek, *The Voice in My Heart* (New York: HarperCollins, 2006), 206.

SEE ::

Watch video session four: SUFFERING

Use streaming instructions on inside cover or DVD.

Take notes if you like.

_____
_____
_____
_____
_____
_____
_____
_____
_____
_____
_____
_____
_____
_____
_____
_____
_____
_____
_____
_____
_____
_____
_____
_____
_____

ASK ::

Use session four: SUFFERING

Conversation Cards for group discussion.

PLACES :: 5

Work through pages 114–133 on your own before your next group meeting and before you watch the next video teaching.

Several years ago, I was introduced to Katie Davis through her blog. She is a young twentysomething, spending her life adopting orphaned girls off the streets of Uganda. Anyone who encounters her life and words goes on to be changed. So our community began to pray about moving to Africa and adopting dozens of children.

Bekah is my spunky, passionate friend who would strip down and offer a homeless person her shirt without thinking, if they asked. So of course Katie's story had her ready to take her three young babies across the world. But at least for the time being, her husband, Brandon, wasn't so sure that stripping in public or the continent of Africa were in their future. So Bekah began to pray. Within days of that surrendered prayer, she was in a coffee shop sharing Christ with a young woman who worked in Brandon's office. Weeks later, she was inviting neighbors to a Bible study in her home. And years later, they can look back and see a trail of loved and changed neighbors and coworkers.

She has used the words *my Africa* many times to describe her neighborhood and Brandon's workplace. It's her mission field.

Marc and Kayan also encountered Katie Davis's blog around the same time we did. They were new believers who had originally attended our church because of the many adoptive families in our church with children from Rwanda; they were adopting from Rwanda too. They say, "Some people find adoption through God. We found God through adoption."

Marc and Kayan sat in the same seats as Brandon and Bekah while my husband preached surrender, and our whole community prayed about "their Africa." Marc, a very respected physician in Austin, began to envision taking his skills in internal medicine and their three babies to Rwanda to train doctors and offer health care to a country in desperate need of it. Kayan was on board. They sold their house in the one of the nicest neighborhoods in Austin and are now preparing for their move to Rwanda in the coming months.

If we are going to think about our purpose, there is no escaping this question: Do we stay in our place, or do we need to go?

Some of you have jobs you hate and will be called to stay, and some of you have jobs you love and will be called to go. The paradigm of a believer is completely different than that of those without God. Without a living God, you get to be your own god. With a living God, who works for eternal purposes, he gets to use us however the heck he pleases.

STUDY ::

Look back at Genesis 39 from last week, and read Genesis 40

Name Joseph's "places" in Genesis 39 and 40.

Describe the amount of control Joseph had over his circumstances (jobs and home) in these decades of his life.

In the description of the time when Joseph was enslaved and in prison, describe what you see about his:

Work ethic

Concern for people

Attitude toward God

Use of his gifts

View of waiting

Study the initiative Joseph takes in these settings. What do you learn as you watch him take initiative?

STUDY MATTHEW 28:16–20

This scripture describes Jesus, just before he ascends to heaven, charging his men (and every one of us that would follow him in every generation) with a job on this earth.

In your own words write our job description from these verses.

LIFE IS TOO SHORT

There is a lot we can know. We know our mission. We know at least a glimpse of the story of God here through Scripture. We know we are to love, without warrant, every person God puts in our path, and we know we are to love God more than all of it. When it comes down to it, 99 percent of being in the will of God is being wholly willing to be in the will of God. God is not vague, even though he can be quiet. He is completely wise in his timing of when he shows his will.

You may need to change your place to be in his will, but to tell you the truth, most of you reading this have enough opportunity for ministry right under your noses that you never need to move or change a thing.

So let's find out. Begin by naming your places. For example, my places are my neighborhood, my kids' school, church, social media, and ministry through speaking and writing.

Jot down some of your places here:

* * *

Years ago when I lived in Austin, there was a popular bumper sticker that read, "Life is too short to live in Dallas." Austinites thought it was funny. Here is my version for our purposes today: life is too short to spend much time worrying about where on this planet you should be. As Jim Elliot, the great martyr missionary, said, "Wherever you are, be all there."[4]

We live in a time in history when job changes, moves, and so on are within reason and perfectly acceptable. So rather than be paralyzed with fear that you might move when you should have stayed or you might stay when you should have moved, pray and commit your ways to the Lord. And then go *do something.*

At times in the past, my view of God's sovereignty over the world, over our stories, has paralyzed me. *If God has a plan, what if I am not in it?*

Now, a better understanding of his sovereignty has helped me move without fear and with tons of freedom. God's will is like a loving dad in a swimming pool asking his little child to jump into his arms. And whether that child jumps really far or barely scoots on his bottom into the pool, that dad will move to catch him. Fear of messing up the will of God will paralyze us. There is no need for that fear. If we will just jump, his will is going to catch us. Let him be God, move ahead with what you know, and quit overanalyzing what you don't.

---

4. Jim Elliot, as quoted by Elisabeth Elliot, *Through Gates of Splendor* (Peabody, MA: Hendrickson Publishers, 1956, 1996), 11.

> Do not be anxious about anything, but in everything, by prayer and petition, with thanksgiving, present your requests to God. And the peace of God, which transcends all understanding, will guard your hearts and your minds in Christ Jesus.
>
> **PHILIPPIANS 4:6–7**

Joseph did this beautifully. God had shown him he would do these awesome things with his life, so rather than worry about being stuck in prison or as a slave, he did great things wherever he was.

Do great works wherever you are. But also do not be afraid to go (and do not be afraid to stay). In heaven, Katie Davis won't be rewarded because of her location on earth; she will be rewarded for her obedience and faithfulness. In the same way, many mothers who worked from home or people who spent most of their lives in cubicles will be standing beside her receiving similar crowns.

It's not our places; it's what we do in our places.

Are you discontent in your places? Write about it.

Do you think this restlessness is discontentment or a restlessness from God wanting to move you toward more?

The above questions are very important and will likely need discussion with family or community around you. But do your best to process the answers because it will help you commit to invest if you can settle into your place.

After Christ gave the Great Commission and ascended to heaven, the apostles got after it, being persecuted as they went. The apostle Paul wrote chapter one of his letter to the Philippians from prison:

WHO ARE YOU, LORD? & WHAT DO YOU WANT FOR ME?

Read Philippians 1:12-26. In light of what you read, answer the questions above.

JUMPING INTO PLACE

You can't read Paul's words and not feel something. I read them and want nothing more than to see Christ made huge through my life, and to see Christ preached. It is so clear, for at least a minute, that Christ and his kingdom are all that matter in this life.

I want to come to the end of my life and see how God was able to move into time and space through me. I want to see many moments that will last forever, many moments when I sat in boring or painful places that I preached anyway. I want moments that no one else saw but that God used to build his kingdom. If I am to go on living and breathing here, I want it to be worth it.

I want to be:

:: all in and more concerned with people than places;

:: more concerned with what God could do through me than my comfort or position in this life;

:: jumping in with all my might not for some big splash but because I am jumping toward my God and his perfect plan for me.

I am confident in this: he will be there to catch me.

What if we made decisions in our lives based on how we could most effectively show Christ to this world?

VISION

Write your places in the left-hand column of the graph below. Pray about your places, asking for wisdom, guidance, and vision.

After praying and giving it some thought, fill in the next column with a possible vision for each place. How might God want you to be intentional like Joseph in each place?

YOUR PLACES	A VISION

DREAM

Are you feeling free or moved to change any of your places? It's okay to consider that possibility every once in a while. Every year, Zac and I pray and ask God if we are where he wants us to be. Are we called to move or change anything? It keeps our hands open and allows God to move us if he wills.

So lay your places before God, writing a prayer below each one. (If you are married, include your spouse in this.)

City

Neighborhood

Jobs

Schools

Other places

DEAL

Recently I was talking with a girl who wept because she wanted a life of purpose. I asked what she did, and she told me she was developing a sex education program that might be used in the entire Texas school district. *Um* . . . I was confused. How could she *not* feel purpose in this God-given place? She went on to realize that there was certainly purpose there, but she was living in so much fear that she would fail at this huge task that she couldn't embrace her place.

Maybe you are exactly in the will of God, living a life of purpose, but you can't even see it because you are afraid.

Afraid your place doesn't matter. Afraid you won't succeed. Afraid God doesn't see you. Afraid that what you're doing isn't specifically ministry. Afraid what people will think if you live for Christ in your place.

What about your place makes you afraid?

Now preach to yourself. Take each fear, and combat it with the biblical truth below. You may find it helpful to get input from trusted friends here.

Ladies, it's time to get over it. Do not let fear distract you from living boldly in your places.

For God has not given us a spirit of fear and timidity, but of power, love, and self-discipline.

2 TIMOTHY 1:7 NLT

DRAW

Draw a picture of your neighborhood, dorm, or apartment complex, and write about the lives near you and what you know about them. Do they have kids or a dog? What do they do? What do they care about?

How could you bring your places together? Dinner or a game night? Or hanging out on the back porch? I bet they will come. Be brave, pray, and take initiative.

CONCLUSION

Mary embraced me the moment we met in our mutual friend's home. She sat me down and held both of my hands, eager to tell me her story and how it intersected with mine. She had recently moved with her new husband out to his country home on the outskirts of Austin. Mary insisted on meeting every neighbor, even though houses sat acres apart. But as years went by, it started to seem like so much trouble to walk all that way, and potentially creepy to drive up to their front doors.

But as she prayed a prayer of surrender, she knew God was telling her to take him to her spread-out country neighborhood. So she decided to host a *Stuck* study and wrote individual, handwritten letters to each neighbor inviting them to come. Immediately she gathered fifteen women who were hungry for connection and over a year later they are still meeting and studying the Bible.

Our places are not an accident. Your gifts and stories will be used in many different places over your lifetime. We have freedom to dream about our places; there is great purpose in using our gifts in corporations, nonprofits, state school systems, churches, and neighborhoods. Our God does not separate secular and spiritual. He just wants you to participate in his story wherever you are and with whatever you have.

If we each played our part, from Africa to Dallas, we would get to heaven and know that in our little place, we were a part of something too big to ever conceive of while we were here.

Because, you know, we aren't really in our true "place" yet. The place we were made for is coming; no place feels quite right until we are home.

Those the LORD has rescued will return. They will enter Zion with singing; everlasting joy will crown their heads. Gladness and joy will overtake them, and sorrow and sighing will flee away.

ISAIAH 51:11

SEE ::

Watch video session five: PLACES

Use streaming instructions on inside cover or DVD.

Take notes if you like.

ASK ::

Use session five: PLACES

Conversation Cards for group discussion.

PEOPLE :: 6

GOD'S STORY

Work through pages 138–157 on your own before your next
group meeting and before you watch the next video teaching.

One night, Zac and I found ourselves absorbed in a documentary called *Babies*. The documentary follows the first year of life of four babies in different parts of the world.

There is no talking, no plot, no story. And you *cannot quit watching*. An African baby crawling through the mud outside his hut, a baby in urban Tokyo juggling the pressures of, you know, being a baby in urban Tokyo, a Mongolian farm baby taking a bath with the family goat, and an American "green" baby living the life of a hippie.

Watching these babies come into their spot on the planet, you cannot help but think, *There are not accidents or coincidences.* There is a God setting us in our time and place with our people. And if that is true, he has a plan for it all.

Imagine getting to heaven and God saying:

> Before I laid the foundations of the earth, I thought of you and of the days you would live on earth. I planned out the people and the places I would give you. I laid out your neighbors and your workplace, the places you would attend school, and your family; I laid out enough days to do all the good works that I purposed for you, and I equipped you with all you would need to accomplish those purposes here. I filled you with my Spirit to encourage and remind you and lead you. I gave you my Word so you would know me and know what to do. I gave you people to run with and people who needed me.
>
> Let's talk about how all that went.

I shudder to think how accidental we tend to believe life is.

My good friend has died twice. Julie was resuscitated both times, but due to a heart condition, she could die again at any point. She doesn't live like anyone else I know. She doesn't waste time with small talk. And no one wastes time with her, because life feels short.

Julie is thirty-five and has two young boys who know how to dial 911. But Julie is not afraid.

Before any knowledge of her faulty heart, Julie trained and became a pediatric cardiologist RN. Last week I walked into an enormous room as Julie shared about her heart and death and faith to a room full of men and women in the cardiology community.

Dare you tell me that is all an accident?

I know your life may feel more random and disconnected than Julie's, but you cannot hear her story and tell me God didn't orchestrate the good and the bad to intersect in rooms like I just saw. And you also can't tell me that he would plan the details of Julie's and Joseph's lives and ignore yours.

He is big enough to plot the number of stars and your hairs, and he is big enough to plot your life. He is intentional about who he lays in your path. And you better believe it breaks his heart when we think otherwise.

Here is the thing about Joseph. He could not control his circumstances, but he intentionally leveraged every relationship in his path for the glory of God. Despite the chaos of his circumstances and the incredible evil brought against him by people he trusted, he never quit choosing to trust and love people. He never wasted opportunity to serve—even those who wronged him.

STUDY ::

Read Genesis 41–45

Before you respond to these chapters in Genesis, look back at Joseph's life in slavery and prison and describe the people who surrounded him. Then describe how he treated them.

In the chapters you just read, where do you see Joseph's trust in God play out?

Describe Joseph's attitude toward Pharaoh.

Describe Joseph's commitment to his family.

Describe Joseph's love for people on earth in his generation. (Genesis 45:3–11)

Describe what you learn about God's purposes in this story.

As you process your life and people, what is God showing you as you study Joseph's story? Do you respond to your people in a similar or different way than he did?

STUDY MARK 12:28-34

Describe our first and second callings as followers of Christ here and now.

1. _____

_____

_____

2. _____

_____

_____

Now write about what that looks like in the context of your life today.

GREAT INVESTMENTS

If we are honest, we'll admit that it is hard to love God and it is hard to love people. So you know what we tend to do instead of doing the difficult work of loving them? We piddle.

To piddle is to waste time, or spend one's time idly or inefficiently. It is easier to survive this life on the surface, bumping up against people gently than do the mess of intentionally loving them. Love takes risk. Love takes forgiveness and grace. Love takes effort, time, and a commitment to not bolting when it gets hard (because it will get hard).

If this is the cost of deep relationships, we can't possibly have capacity and space to go deep with everyone. So we have to become intentional.

WHO DO YOU NEED?

We need people to help us love God.

> But you, O Lord, are a shield about me, my glory, and the lifter of my head.
>
> **PSALM 3:3** ESV

We all forget. We forget that God is real and that life is short. And we forget that how we run this race matters. So we need people to be for us what Julie is for me: someone who will place their fingers under our chins and lift our heads. I need perspective as I run. I get tired and want to quit. I need people ahead of me, shouting back that it is worth it. We need deep kindred souls beside us, making the run more fun and helping us to not feel crazy and alone.

We need people. We need the *right* people. And sometimes finding the right people takes discipline and effort. When we find those right people, we have to fight for them. We have to prioritize time and issue grace over and over, because every human on this earth will disappoint us. And when that happens, we love and fight for them even harder.

We all fell in love with shows like *Friends*, because we deeply want to have "our people." Close friends and mentors don't fall into our laps. You search and invest, and then you allow them to be imperfect versions of what you were hoping for in your head. Most of us are waiting to be invited, waiting to be pursued, waiting for friends to come to us.

> Put on then, as God's chosen ones, holy and beloved, compassionate hearts, kindness, humility, meekness, and patience, bearing with one another and, if one has a complaint against another, forgiving each other; as the Lord has forgiven you, so you also must forgive. And above all these put on love, which binds everything together in perfect harmony. And let the peace of Christ rule in your hearts, to which indeed you were called in one body. And be thankful.
>
> **COLOSSIANS 3:12–15** ESV

Love is such an active process, and we are fairly lazy. So initiate. Then when you come together, initiate depth. Great conversations come from great questions and honest answers. Become someone who does both well. One of the ways I grow and experience God is over Mexican food with kindred friends talking about deep things.

Who do you need? Who are your mission-minded, like-minded friends? Who are the people who make you love God more? Who can you safely share your soul with?

Who are wiser mentors you could pursue?

Who needs you?

> While Jesus was having dinner at Levi's house, many tax collectors and sinners were eating with him and his disciples, for there were many who followed him. When the teachers of the law who were Pharisees saw him eating with the sinners and tax collectors, they asked his disciples: "Why does he eat with tax collectors and sinners?"
>
> On hearing this, Jesus said to them, "It is not the healthy who need a doctor, but the sick. I have not come to call the righteous, but sinners."
>
> **MARK 2:15–17**

Now it is our turn to be Jesus to this world. We exist for God and for those who need God. Within the church, we use our gifts to build up and equip the body. Outside of the church, we show love to show God.

Next time you are in a public space, be awkward and look in people's eyes. People, nearly every one of them, are hurting, even if they don't say it. And we hold armfuls of their cure.

We get God, and we get to give God away; it is for our joy. I am never more content than when I am meeting need.

In the movie *Amazing Grace*, William Pitt's character races barefoot through a field with William Wilberforce and says to him "Why is it you only feel the thorns in your feet when you stop running?"[5]

When we run for God and for people, we forget for just a moment about ourselves, and it feels amazing. Nothing makes a soul sicker than too much time given to itself.

Together Wilberforce and Pitt, who became the prime minister of England, spent their lives fighting the slave trade in England. Their friendship was God-ordained for a purpose. You will never grow closer to people than you do when you live on a mission together.

SO WHO NEEDS GOD AROUND YOU?

Pray.
Pursue them.
Ask them great questions.
Share your struggles and your God.
Dream of ways you can meet their needs.

There will be people you know who need you. But also seek out relationships with people outside your circles. Some of my favorite moments in my life have happened as I have stepped out of my comfort zone. Like taking some women from a local halfway house out to bowl with some of my friends. I remember sitting in a bowling alley with a woman just out of prison who exuded more joy than I remember ever feeling in my life.

---

5. Michel Apted, director, *Amazing Grace* (20th Century Fox, 2007).

She was about to see her kids, and it had been years. Her joy and perspective changed me—and I needed to be changed. God's economy makes beautiful exchanges: as we give, we grow.

Seek the uncomfortable. Life is short, and it is worth the risk. You do not risk like a fool; you are wisely investing in the only two things that will not die: God and people. No better reason to make piddling a thing of the past.

WHO ARE YOU, LORD? & WHAT DO YOU WANT FOR ME?

Read Hebrews 10:19-25, 32-26. In light of what you read, answer the questions above.

CONSIDER

Dream about people you know in each category listed in the chart below. Then consider a plan to intentionally pursue them.

PEOPLE YOU NEED	PLAN FOR TIME TOGETHER
Mentors	
Friends	
Family	
Other	

PEOPLE WHO NEED YOU	PLAN FOR TIME TOGETHER
Neighbors	
Coworkers	
Friends	
Family	
Outside of acquaintances (prison, elderly, poor)	
Other	

PROJECT :: 1

ACT

Have an intentional conversation this week with someone you do not know. It can be at a restaurant, at school or work, in your neighborhood, or any of your other places. Brainstorm some conversation-starting questions first:

Find places of common ground and vulnerably share about your struggles and where God meets you in them. Write about your experiences below.

Where is the most natural place for you to engage people who may need God?

DEAL

Which of the following is keeping you from meaningful friendships: (1) time, (2) fear, (3) insecurity, (4) expectations, (5) distraction, (6) other? Write about it.

Which of the following is keeping you from engaging in relationships with those who need God: (1) time, (2) fear, (3) insecurity, (4) expectations, (5) distraction, (6) other? How?

LIST

Narrow down a list of five names of people you need:

1. _____
2. _____
3. _____
4. _____
5. _____

Narrow down a list of five names of people who need you:

1. _____
2. _____
3. _____
4. _____
5. _____

How can you begin to invest more in these people? What are some practical ways you can keep all your time from going to casual friendships?

CONCLUSION

Two years ago, Julie and I sat on her back porch bringing in the New Year with our husbands and other friends. We sat overlooking the Austin skyline and dreaming about what the new year could hold. Dreaming with friends who may die causes you to dream the best kind of dreams— the very most important kinds of dreams.

Julie sat silent. I didn't know why. It turns out she was scared, because she was being led to share her story with the wider world. Here are her words:

> I began to pray that the Lord would bring an opportunity for me to share. I did not expect the opportunities to be big or grand; rather I just expected to have one-on-one conversations with people.
>
> I began to share more openly with our friends, and then with my coworkers, neighbors, and even patients. Then, the Go Red heart campaign reached out to me and asked me to share my story at their national events. Our church, Austin Stone, put together a little film which has now been viewed by people living in countries all across the globe. God has used my struggle to reach people who need him—who need hope.
>
> The Lord has given each of us a story. It is the story of how he uniquely and purposefully pursues us to restore our souls for his name and renown.

Who needs you? Who needs God? Who needs hope?

SEE ⠃

Watch video session six: PEOPLE

Use streaming instructions on inside cover or DVD.

Take notes if you like.

ASK ::

Use session six: PEOPLE

Conversation Cards for group discussion.

PASSIONS :: 7

Work through pages 164–177 on your own before your next group meeting and before you watch the next video teaching.

William Wilberforce knew his passion. He resisted it, but this passion held him captive as a young man, nearly at the same time that he became completely captivated by Jesus. He met God and wanted nothing more than to begin vocational ministry; he was convinced this was the best way to serve God. But the passion that kept him up at night, that had him pacing floors and banging tables, was the unacceptable injustice of the slave trade in England.

His minister, John Newton, a former slave trader, enlightened him about the horrors of slavery. William was haunted. God had given him a gift for communication, the empathy of one who had suffered, a position of influence through the House of Commons, and a deep, lifelong friendship with the prime minister of England. And he was faced with a need too awful to ignore. A dozen or more threads, ordained by the hand of God, were slowly assembling into a great calling.

Finally Wilberforce's friends convinced him that God could potentially use him most in the place of a politician. He ran headfirst toward the thing that haunted him. It was painful, and most of his life was spent before there was any reform.[6]

But at some point William's passions turned into a calling. When that happens, the cost becomes irrelevant.

---

6. Eric Metaxas, *Amazing Grace* (New York: HarperCollins, 2007).

We all are longing to live for something bigger than ourselves. As believers in Jesus Christ with need all around us, we get to. We look past the normal of mundane jobs and boring places and see the need in them, and passions start to wake up. God built us to take the material around us and invest it into our nearest need. But sometimes it's hard to see the need around us.

It's easy to miss the point of the story of Joseph. What was God doing through Joseph's decades of suffering and the betrayal of his family and the unique gifts that he possessed? Yes, he was refining Joseph. Yes, he was restoring Joseph to his family. Yes, he was using him throughout Egypt in many people's lives. But ultimately God intended Joseph's life to *save* many lives. With the famine coming, God would use the faith and obedience of one to save them all.

Every one of us who knows Christ has this as the foundational calling of our lives. William Wilberforce and Joseph aren't especially epic, they just gave their lives to the problem of their generations. We could do that too. And together as one body with many parts, we could see God move.

STUDY ::

Reread Genesis 41:41–56

Describe Joseph's mission at this point:

Describe the faith that Joseph had to have in God to prepare Egypt in this way:

READ GENESIS 47:13–31

Describe Joseph's job.

Describe the way Joseph led through the famine.

What motivated Joseph? What were some of his passions in these verses?

How were the people around Joseph influenced by his leadership?

THE ROOT OF PASSION

The word *passion* originates in the Latin word meaning "to suffer," referring to Christ's sufferings on the cross. Passions have become nearly synonymous with pleasures in modern culture. But when we consider that passion is originally defined as the moment of the deepest suffering of Christ for our good, it lifts the word from human desires to a monumental love willing to suffer.

God often leads us to passions through suffering experienced or perceived. Weeks ago, as you considered your scars, hopefully passions began to arise out of your darkest moments. You long to give the world what you failed to receive. But passions are also born out of observing suffering.

William Wilberforce observed suffering in the slave trade, and as it haunted him, his passion followed with a great intensity that eventually led him to his calling. Joseph suffered great pain in his life, but his suffering gave him a sincere passion for reconciliation and human care. We don't naturally have passion for others. We are naturally danged selfish.

But when we were bought by Christ, we exchanged our heart full of self-seeking passions for things on this earth for God's heart. And now we share his passions.

> I will cleanse you from all your impurities and from all your idols. I will give you a new heart and put a new spirit in you; I will remove from you your heart of stone and give you a heart of flesh. And I will put my Spirit in you and move you to follow my decrees and be careful to keep my laws.
>
> **EZEKIEL 36:25–27**

Our hearts are new, and now what was cold and hard is soft and full of compassion, led and moved by his Spirit.

Just because God loves us and wanted to make life more fun, he built us to love different things so we could meet different needs. So my daughter Kate loves art, and Caroline would rather sing, and my son Conner is smarter than most humans on earth, and Coop may be the next Emmitt Smith. And every one of them can pursue these passions for the glory of God and the love of people. Joseph and William Wilberforce pursued their gifts and passions through worldly jobs for the glory of God and the good of people.

It's beautiful that your heart doesn't beat fast about the same things my heart beats over. It's beautiful that your gifts are not the same as your mom's, and your place is not the same as your best friend's. When we start to lay out our threads, it is unbelievable—breathtaking, really—to see how what felt average about ourselves weeks ago starts to take on intricate beauty. Our untangling threads reveal God's sovereignty and attention to detail. Beautiful is the body of Christ stretched and poured out into every crevice of this world, every city, every neighborhood, every office, every home. It's the unselfish passions of people displaying the love of their God in a million unique ways.

> The place God calls you to is the place where your deep gladness and the world's deep hunger meet.
>
> **FREDERICK BUECHNER** [2]

It's beautiful that all your unique threads run in a direction that blesses people and shows God. That direction is usually determined by the things that cause you to beat the table, or lay in bed awake, or speak with exclamation marks.

Our passions determine our direction. We began this journey in hopes of discovering how to invest our lives. I promised no magical writing in the sky—only a journey to discover more of God and the pieces of life he gave you to make him known. Where does your heart bleed for the need you see around you?

2. Frederick Buechner, *Wishful Thinking* (New York: HarperOne,1993).

WHO ARE YOU, LORD? & WHAT DO YOU WANT FOR ME?

Read Hebrews 12:1-3. In light of what you read, answer the questions above.

CONSIDER

What need do you see around you?

When have you seen need that made your heart race?

When you get mad about injustice, what is it?

When do you remember meeting a need and feeling very fulfilled?

What do you think your main passions in life are currently?

FIGHT

Nothing kills passion more than the fear of man, whether a quest for approval or nagging comparison. The biggest enemy to passion is entangling yourself in pleasing people.

How have you seen your passion affected by people (externally) or self-comparison (internally)? Chart a few of your main passions below, and then write out how they can be affected in the columns below.

YOUR PASSIONS	APPROVAL OF MAN	COMPARISON
_____	_____	_____
	_____	_____
	_____	_____
_____	_____	_____
	_____	_____
	_____	_____
_____	_____	_____
	_____	_____
	_____	_____
_____	_____	_____
	_____	_____
	_____	_____
_____	_____	_____
	_____	_____

DREAM

Don't be afraid to do what you love for God's glory, even though it may seem like a "nonspiritual" thing.

What do you love to do? What do you enjoy?

Dream of ways you could use those passions for God's glory or people's flourishing, now, soon, and in the long term.

ACT

Often we protect our lives from observing the need around us. With your small group, dream of a need in your community, and together organize a time for you to serve that need.

Some examples may be visiting a retirement home, serving in a soup kitchen, organizing a dinner to get to know neighbors, sponsoring a child together. Outline these dreams in the space below.

Now pray together these interactions will spark something for God's glory.

CONCLUSION

> Everything that does not come from faith is sin.
>
> **ROMANS 14:23**

This is a verse that makes every one of us shudder and consider ourselves the worst of sinners. How does everything come from a place of faith? We all doubt and get fearful and wander toward lives completely absorbed with ourselves. Hear this. We are unable to move without God. He moves us; we just have to let him. He breathes faith into us, and only then do we move.

If you are anxious because you don't know your passions or don't know if you are living them or ever could, stop.

We cannot love.
We cannot know God.
We cannot know ourselves.
We cannot change.
We cannot bleed for others.

We cannot *move* without God's Spirit moving in and through us to accomplish his purposes. We are not left as orphans to figure all this out. He is with us. That is why Jesus could say, "My yoke is easy and my burden is light" (Matthew 11:30). Because he didn't call us to something alone. He carries the yoke for us.

We run with his strength, vision, heart, and power.

SEE ::

Watch video session seven: PASSIONS

Use streaming instructions on inside cover or DVD.

Take notes if you like.

ASK ::

Use session seven: PASSIONS

Conversation Cards for group discussion.

MYSTERY :: 8

Work through pages 184–203 on your own before your next group meeting and before you watch the final video teaching.

Along with most of the world, in spring 2013 we were watching *The Bible* series on the History Channel. Seeing the reality of what these moments may have been like has changed me. Watching Jesus choose fasting in the desert for forty days and nights alone, all I could think was, *You are God! Why are you doing this to yourself? You do not need extra power when you are the Son of God! Does your Spirit really need to be strengthened and prepared for what is ahead?*

In the dramatization, right after Jesus walks out of the wilderness having resisted the devil, he prepares to begin his ministry and he closes his eyes. My daughter was watching with me and asked, "Mom, what is he doing?"

I said, through tears, "He's praying, baby."

And I cry again as I write this because while I have read at least dozens of times that Jesus prayed, to see him pray broke me down. Our Savior, fully God, depended on his Father for every breath. He never acted apart from God's will, never acted in his flesh, never bowed down to any earthly desire. He wanted so much to live out his Father's will that he subjected himself to forty days without food or people. And then to much worse on the cross. It was so humble and right. Jesus knew there was a war, and the war was for us. We were to be won back, and he would choose suffering again and again until he had gotten us back.

His eyes close, and Jesus, my Lord and Savior, prays.

Are we above such dependence? And yet how many days do I act as if I am?

God's goal for our lives is that we would live in complete and utter surrender and dependence on him. He built us to need him. And it is *always* his mercy to show us that need, whatever the cost.

So as we process how we each spend our lives while we are here, know that nothing we have done together matters without the Spirit of God. He illuminates our understanding of God and of ourselves, and he leads us daily. He empowers every move we will make for his glory. He is God in us, with us, for us, through us. I do not want to spend one fleeting day here without embracing as much of God as I can on earth.

> Flesh gives birth to flesh, but the Spirit gives birth to spirit. You should not be surprised at my saying, "You must be born again." The wind blows wherever it pleases. You hear its sound, but you cannot tell where it comes from or where it is going. So it is with everyone born of the Spirit.
>
> **JOHN 3:6–8**

When Jesus saves, we have full access to his Spirit. We have a regenerate soul.

Regenerate (adj.)
1. formed or created again
2. spiritually reborn or converted
3. restored to a better, higher, or more worthy state[7]

---

7. Merriam-Webster Online, s.v. "regenerate," accessed June 4, 2013, http://www.merriam-webster.com/dictionary/regenerate.

It is an odd word, but it is one of my favorite words because of the fact that the insides of me are completely reborn, new, different. That is the evidence of my salvation; it is the evidence of God in me, and it is the only foundation from which we can dream of pleasing God. It takes away the striving and comparing I can tend to turn to in this life.

Without a new soul, without the Spirit filling us, we are just jacked-up, stuck humans.

But with his Spirit . . .

If we only had an inkling of all we miss because we do not pray, because we do not believe the Spirit in us is able to do impossible things, we would shudder. You have God in you and waiting to go crazy through you, if you will just let him.

Apart from me you can do nothing.

JOHN 15:5

STUDY ::

Read Luke 24:44–49

This was a big moment. Jesus was telling his men exactly what had just happened, and he connected it to the prophecies. He also gave them instruction on how to now proceed. In this one little paragraph, there was so much for these men to take in.

Write down each fact and command that Jesus revealed in these verses.

Why do you think he warned them about moving forward without his Spirit?

READ ACTS 2

Describe what the Spirit brings to us.

Describe the Spirit's power in verses 17 to 21.

Describe Jesus from these verses.

Describe the call of God through Peter in verses 38 and 39.

Describe the lives of the people who had received the Spirit in verses 42 to 47.

RESTLESS FOR GOD

We do not have power to change souls. We do not have power to change our own soul or to change others. And at times that concept has crippled and frustrated me, until its truth shifted to freedom. I do not want to be responsible for what can only be handled and achieved by God himself.

It is possible that you have, with all your heart, dug into Scripture and prayed for God to show his will and done every project, and you still feel unsure about your purpose. Take comfort. This is a journey that God put into motion, and he knows us well enough to know that he needs to tether us to himself with the unknowns. We get all independent with what we think we know.

This is why he doesn't write in the sky, even though he could. This is why we all still ache a little even when we are running wild with God's purposes for us. He wants us holding on and running with him.

The other day my thirteen-year-old son walked into my room, sat down on the sofa, and said, "Mom, I need to tell you about my day." I immediately assumed he was obligated by the school principal to tell me the trouble he had incurred, but instead he started rambling about his friendships and the girl's heart he recently broke, and he wondered out loud with me how to navigate it all.

My son, for the first time in months, needed me. And he couldn't have done any more spectacular act to show his love for me.

Close your eyes, like Jesus did, and pray. Right now. Wherever you are, tell God you need him. We forget we need him. And the beautiful thing about what we have studied here is that we tend to remember that we need him when we are pouring our lives into his purposes. When we are building for him, his Spirit reminds us we need him every day.

"My grace is sufficient for you, for my power is made perfect in weakness." Therefore I will boast all the more gladly about my weaknesses, so that Christ's power may rest on me.

2 CORINTHIANS 12:9

I remember I need God when:

I feel tangled up with sin and fear.

> For the Spirit God gave us does not make us timid, but gives us power, love and self-discipline.
>
> **2 TIMOTHY 1:7**

I don't know what to do.

> My sheep listen to my voice; I know them, and they follow me.
>
> **JOHN 10:27**

I forget.

> But the Advocate, the Holy Spirit, whom the Father will send in my name, will teach you all things and will remind you of everything I have said to you.
>
> **JOHN 14:26**

I am discouraged.

> In the same way, the Spirit helps us in our weakness. We do not know what we ought to pray for, but the Spirit himself intercedes for us with groans that words cannot express.
>
> **ROMANS 8:26** NIV 1984

We need God. When we are restless, bored, numb, cold, selfish, or distracted, it won't be some great vision that will fill our souls; it will be the Spirit of the living God who fills our souls. He alone will fill us. As we experience wholeness, we will be impassioned to run our guts out, giving him away with our stories, passions, and gifts to our people in our places. Run. Do not grow weary for there is a day coming when you will face God, and honestly it will be here before we know it.

God doesn't change the world through grand visions; he changes the world through surrendered people hungry for his glory.

STUDY

WHO ARE YOU, LORD? & WHAT DO YOU WANT FOR ME?

Read Romans 8:1-7. In light of what you read, answer the questions above.

BELIEVE

So then, those who are in the flesh cannot please God. But you are not in the flesh but in the Spirit, if indeed the Spirit of God dwells in you. Now if anyone does not have the Spirit of Christ, he is not His.

ROMANS 8:8–9 NKJV

Do not leave this process without this one thing perfectly clear in your mind: Have you put your faith in the person and work of Jesus Christ for the forgiveness of sin?

If so, you are full of the Spirit of God, whether you feel him or not. He is promised to you, and your soul is reborn, different, new, free from the bondage of sin, and free to spend your life on the purposes of God that will never fade.

If not, what is holding you back?

If so, how can you live more in the truth of what God's Spirit does for you?

Get with someone from your small group or a friend who knows God and process this. What you believe about God is the most important thing about you.

THREADS

The time has come to look at the complete picture. You have dug deep, been vulnerable, and opened yourself up to new possibilities.

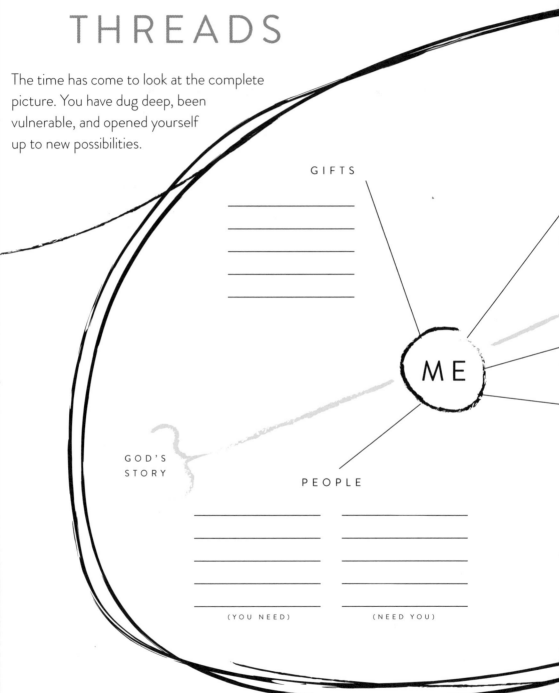

GIFTS

ME

GOD'S STORY

PEOPLE

(YOU NEED) (NEED YOU)

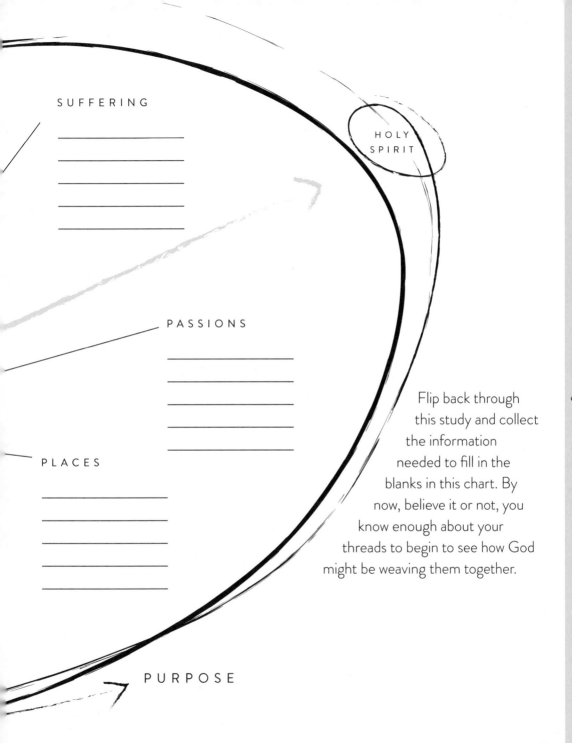

SUFFERING

_____
_____
_____
_____

PASSIONS

_____
_____
_____
_____

PLACES

_____
_____
_____
_____

PURPOSE

HOLY SPIRIT

Flip back through this study and collect the information needed to fill in the blanks in this chart. By now, believe it or not, you know enough about your threads to begin to see how God might be weaving them together.

GATHER

Gather together at a dinner with a few friends or with your small group. Each of you should bring along the final threads chart you just completed. First pray for discernment, and then ask each other these questions:

What connections do you see as you look at my threads?

What ideas do you have for me as I dream about ways God could use all of this?

What do you think is unique about what God has given me?

What could my next steps be?

Where do you sense me holding back?

RESPOND

Respond to God about this journey. Write a letter to him thanking him for what he has done in and through you. Lay out your threads and pray over them. Commit them to him. Tell him if you are willing to use your life and all that he has given you for his glory. Ask him how he wants you to use your threads.

_____
_____
_____
_____
_____
_____
_____
_____
_____
_____
_____
_____
_____
_____
_____
_____
_____
_____
_____
_____
_____
_____

PROJECT :: 4

CONCLUSION

How do we know the will of God?

I know you may have come on this journey hoping for complete clarity. You aren't alone. I long for clarity because God keeps asking me to trust him and to risk. And it is painful. It would seem so much easier if he would just spell things out a bit. But as we all walk by faith, we are tasting more of him.

I do not know what you will do when you close this book, but I trust fully in the promise of Scripture that if you commit all of your ways to the Lord, he will set your path straight (Proverbs 3:6). For me, that has typically looked like only knowing the exact next step on the path and learning to trust him with the darkness ahead.

The restlessness we feel is not a bad thing. I believe it is the longing and passion in us for God—for more. It could push us to move forward, to live epic lives that were designed before the foundations of the earth were laid.

The stirrings of a revolution are in the works. God is gathering a force, and change is coming. It comes from him. But a lot of us, if we're honest, are afraid. We hold close to our chest the new and scary and uncomfortable visions that may just be from God and play a small part in something bigger.

But we need each other.

We need some understanding of ourselves and the empty places around us.

But mostly we just need faith in a real, unseen God.

I believe that together, if we all will quit comparing ourselves to others and just follow our Jesus, something is going to happen. A generation who has quietly been reading and longing and dreaming and falling in love with God is about to wake up. We are about to let God run wild through us.

We live once, and then we meet God. We want to live lives that matter for eternal things. We want to be a generation who followed with reckless abandon a God who was real to us.

So let's get after it.

SEE ::

Watch video session eight: MYSTERY

Use streaming instructions on inside cover or DVD.

Take notes if you like.

ASK ::

Use session eight: MYSTERY

Conversation Cards for group discussion.

HOW TO FIND GOD

I can't imagine a more restless feeling than being unsure about the meaning of life and the future of my soul. As long as we are on this earth, we will ache for something bigger, because we were designed for something bigger—something better. We are designed for an intimate relationship with God forever.

Saint Augustine said, "You have made us for yourself, and our hearts are restless until they find their rest in you."[8]

We had a perfect relationship with God until sin entered the world through Adam and Eve. And with sin came the promise of death and eternal separation from God. But from the moment of the first sin, God issued a promise that would bring us back to him.

The penalty had to be paid.

Our sin was to be placed on a perfect sacrifice. God would send his own blameless, perfect Son to bear our sin and suffer our fate—to get us back.

Jesus came fulfilling thousands of years of prophecy, lived a perfect life, and died a gruesome death, reconciling our payment for our sin. Then after three days, he defeated death and rose from the grave and now is seated with the Father, waiting for us.

---

8. Augustine of Hippo, *Saint Augustine's Confessions,* trans. Albert C. Outler (Mineola, N.Y.: Courier Dover Publications, 2002), 103.

Anyone who accepts the blood of Jesus for the forgiveness of their sin is adopted as a child of God, and issued God's very own Spirit to seal and empower us to live this life for him.

Our souls are restless until they rest in God. We were made for him, and he gave everything so that our souls could finally and forever rest in him.

If you have never trusted Christ for the forgiveness of your sins, you can do that this moment. Just tell him your need for him and tell him of your trust in him as your Lord and Savior.

LEADER'S GUIDE

LEADERS,

I am excited to partner with you in your efforts to pour into the lives of women! I pray that these few short pages will help to equip and prepare you to lead this study. Many of you may have led plenty of groups in the past, or perhaps this is the first you've led. Whichever the case, this is a spiritual calling and you are entering spiritual places with these women— and spiritual callings and places need spiritual power.

My husband, Zac, always says, "Changed lives, change lives." If you are not first aware of your own need for life change, the women around you won't see their need. If you allow God into the inner struggles of your heart, the women following you will be much more likely to let him into theirs. These women do not need to see bright and shiny, perfectly poised people; they need to see people who are a mess and daily dependent on God for their hope and strength.

So, what are we going to do together here?

Every single one of us is designed to fit into a unique space with unique offerings. God's will for each one of us will look different. There is a framework within the commandments of Scripture, and within it we are free to create lives reflecting God and his passions here.

First, we are going to chase down and tackle some of what is holding us back from obedience. Then, in part two, we are going to try to get our heads around God and what he is doing on this earth. Then we will consider exactly what pieces of life God has given you to participate in his story. In part three, we will explore what it looks like to live out our purposes. Throughout, we will look at these heart issues in the life of

Joseph, a man who dreamed God's dreams and lived his part in God's story. Joseph's life, told of throughout Genesis 37 to 50, is the story of a life that at times must have felt wasted, and yet God was working in every moment that felt mundane and unfair and dark.

In the end, this is a book about God. It's about the moment at the end of our lives when we will see him. It's about facing the God of the universe and celebrating with him about the life and resources he gave us while we were here.

And because we all want that moment to go well, this is a book about discovering ourselves and getting over ourselves all at the same time. It's about being brave enough to imagine a better world and how we may be used to make it that way. It's about changing the world and changing diapers. About fears and suffering and joy and gifts. About all that is within our control and how nothing is in our control. It's about vision and obedience.

This is a book about spending our lives completely on the glory of God.

We want to know: "What does God want me to do while I am here?" The answer seems hidden and complicated, yet we must go after it. We must not get to heaven and realize we have lived for all the wrong things.

We must not waste our lives. Let's go.

Together we can learn to let down our guards and go to God humbly. Together we can lead others in the same way. We can do this, together!

Jennie

THE VISION

1. That God and eternity would get bigger and more real in your lives, and that as they do get bigger, you would feel compelled to live for eternity and Jesus Christ more than this short life. More than anything, I want you to fix your eyes on Jesus and fall more deeply in love with him.

2. That you would feel released and convicted to dream with the many unique threads that God has placed in your lives, and that you would each see how valuable and important your part in building the kingdom of God is.

3. That you would speak life and peace and freedom into each other. That you would encourage each other in your uniqueness rather than judge or condemn the different paths God may have each of us running.

In sum, here it is . . . this is my dream: That we would all fix our eyes on Jesus, throw off the small junk that holds us back, and run our marked races, cheering each other on.

Therefore, since we are surrounded by such a great cloud of witnesses, let us throw off everything that hinders and the sin that so easily entangles. And let us run with perseverance the race marked out for us, fixing our eyes on Jesus, the pioneer and perfecter of faith. For the joy set before him he endured the cross, scorning its shame, and sat down at the right hand of the throne of God. Consider him who endured such opposition from sinners, so that you will not grow weary and lose heart.

HEBREWS 12:1–3

The rest of this leader's guide is aimed at equipping you to point the women of your group to God in ways that will change their lives.

PREPARING YOURSELF TO LEAD A GROUP

1. **PRAY:** Pray like the world is ending, pray like this is the last chance for people to know him, pray like your lives and futures depend on it, pray like the future of souls in heaven is at stake . . . pray like you need God.

   Pray for your women:

   :: That God would show them why they are restless, and what their hearts truly long for.

   :: That they would feel safe to open up and process.

   :: That they would want more of God and that God would meet them.

   :: That the conversation would be focused on God.

   :: That we would be humble displays of God's grace to these women.

   :: That God would come and fall on your time together.

   :: That many would come to a saving faith as they see God for who he is.

2. LEAN ON GOD.

Allow the Holy Spirit to lead every moment together. We have provided you with tools that we will discuss in the next section; however, they are only tools to use as the Spirit leads you and your time together. God will have unique agendas for each of your groups as you depend on him. Lean into your own weakness and into his strength and direction.

When Jesus left his disciples to go back to his Father in heaven, he essentially said, "Don't go anywhere until you have the helper I will send you" (see Acts 1:4–5). That helper was the Holy Spirit. We need to obey that same command. We shouldn't begin until we are doing so with the power of the Holy Spirit within us. He is real and available and waiting to flood our lives and the lives of those around us as we serve and speak. But we have to wait for him to speak, ask him if we should speak and what we should speak, and ask him what to do in different situations. God wants us to need him and to depend on his Spirit. If this is not how you live on a daily basis, begin today.

3. BE VULNERABLE.

If you choose not to be vulnerable, no one else will be. If you desire women to feel safe with you and your group, be vulnerable. This is not an optional assignment. This is your calling as you lead these women.

4. **LISTEN, BUT ALSO LEAD.** Listen as women share struggles. Some women are taking a tremendous risk in being vulnerable with you. Protect them by not interrupting but by empathizing instead. Do not feel the need to speak after each person shares. After most women have shared their answers to a question, turn it back to the scripture from the study guide and help them process the truth and hope in their struggles. Avoid lecturing, but do bring the women back to truth.

5. **MODEL TRUST.** Be the example. Apply what you have learned and are learning through the study.

THE STUDY

SESSION TOOLS, HOW TO USE THEM, AND FORMAT

This study is uniquely designed to work in any venue or location. I envision women leading this in their homes, on campuses, even in their workplaces. Church buildings are the traditional format for group Bible studies and *Restless* will be effective within the church walls, but the bigger dream is that women would find this study useful in reaching their friends, neighbors, and coworkers.

Whether you find yourself with 150 women in a church auditorium or with a few neighbors in your living room, this study is designed for small groups of women to process truth within their souls.

Because of the depth of the questions and topics, it is essential your group be small enough to share. A maximum of eight women in each group is ideal, but fewer is preferable. If you are in a larger group, divide into smaller groups with volunteer facilitators. With the help of the leader's guide and the Ask conversation cards, those smaller groups should still prove successful with a little support.

TOOLS NEEDED

STUDY GUIDE. Each study guide comes with leader's guide and streaming video access. Every participant will need a Bible study guide. Distribute the books at your first group meeting, or have participants purchase and bring their guides on their own.

CONVERSATION CARD DECK. Group discussion questions and memory verse card for each session.

HOW TO USE YOUR TOOLS

Each lesson is divided into three main sections:

STUDY

Point out the weekly Study section, followed by the Projects. The lessons in the study guide (except for the Getting Started lesson) are meant to be completed during the week before coming to the group meeting. Each week begins with a short intro before. The Study portion is followed by four application projects, then closing thoughts from me.

These lessons may feel different from studies you have done in the past. They are very interactive. The goal of the curriculum is to lead women to dig deeply into Scripture and uncover how it applies to their lives, to deeply engage the mind and the heart. Projects, stories, and Bible study all play a role. The projects in the study guide will provide several options for applying Scripture. You and your group members may be drawing or journaling or engaging in some other activity in these projects. At the group meeting, discuss your experience in working through the lesson.

SEE

Watch the short, engaging video teaching to introduce the lesson via streaming or DVD to set the tone for your time together, and challenge your group to apply Scripture. If your group members want to take notes, encourage them to use the Notes page opposite each SEE title page. Each study guide includes instructions for personal access to streaming video on the inside front cover. This is perfect for anyone who might miss a group gathering, want to rewatch any of the video teaching, or if your group needs to meet on shortened time.

ASK

After the video teaching is complete, ask the group if anything in particular stood out while you prepare the Conversation Cards. The Conversation Cards provide a unique way to jump-start honest discussion. Each week's cards are labeled with the appropriate lesson title and can be used after the video or teaching time. The following is a suggested step-by-step way to use the cards.

:: Begin by laying out the Scripture Cards for that specific week.

:: Direct each group member to take a card.

:: Go over the Ground Rules each week. (Ground rules are found on page 12 and on the back of the Instruction card.)

:: Take turns presenting the question on each card to the group.

Provide adequate time for everyone in your group to respond to each question. Don't feel pressured to read and answer every card. Be sensitive to the leading of the Holy Spirit and your time constraints. Remind the group that what they share and how they share are entirely personal decisions. No one should be forced to answer every card.

NOTE: Make use of this leader's guide to facilitate a great Bible study experience for your group. It will help you point people to the overarching theme for each lesson and will give you specific suggestions on how to share the truth and foster discussion.

SESSION FORMAT

This eight-week study is designed to go deep very quickly. Since women are busy and have full lives, the beauty of this study is it can be led in a living room over a one-hour lunch, or in a church Bible study spread out over two and a half hours. If you have the flexibility, extend the time of sharing in small groups. A frequent complaint is, "We wish we had more time to share." When the group is given deep questions and space to reflect and respond, you'll be surprised how beautiful and plentiful the conversations will be.

These tools are meant to have some flexibility. Here are some suggestions for how to structure your meeting to get the most out of your time together. However, you will be the best judge of what works for your group and the time you have together. Based on your group's needs, choose any combination of going through the questions mixed with reflections from group members' personal study.

OPEN—Personal study discussion [20–35 MINUTES]:

After welcoming everyone and opening in prayer, you may choose to begin by having the women discuss their personal reflections as they have worked through the study guide and Scripture that week. If you have more than eight members, break into small groups for this discussion time before reconvening for the video/teaching time.

SEE—Video teaching [20 MINUTES]:

Watch the video teaching using the streaming code and instructions on the inside front cover of each guide. Use the video teaching to provide a foundation for that week's lesson and to help transition to the group discussion based on the Conversation Cards. Each video is approximately twenty minutes long. If you are supplying teaching in addition to the videos, we recommend you begin with your teaching and then play the video.

NOTE TO CHURCH GROUPS: Due to the nature of this study, we strongly suggest that each group have no more than eight to twelve women and that you have a kit for each group.

ASK—Group Discussion [30–75 MINUTES]:

Especially if there are more than eight group members, divide into smaller groups and have women engage conversation using the ASK: Conversation Card deck. Each lesson has 12 questions on individual cards to select from and are labeled with the appropriate lesson title. This will be a time of deep sharing and discussion that is important to understanding how to apply all that has been learned that week. If your small group needs an extra deck of Ask cards, they are available for purchase at www.thomasnelson.com from your favorite online retailer.

CLOSE—Closing [5–10 MINUTES]:

Pray as a group and encourage everyone to engage in the Study and Projects for the upcoming lesson before meeting again.

TIPS FOR LEADING YOUR GROUP

GUIDING CONVERSATION

You may come across some challenges when leading a group conversation. Normally these challenges fall into two categories. In both situations people will need encouragement and grace from you as a leader. As with everything in this study, seek the Holy Spirit's guidance as you interact with your group members.

DOMINATING THE CONVERSATION: If one
woman seems to be dominating the conversation or going into detail that makes the rest of the group uncomfortable, gently interrupt her if necessary and thank her for sharing. Avoid embarrassing her in front of the group. Ask if there is anyone else who would like to share in response to the original question asked (not to necessarily respond to the woman who was just speaking). If the problem persists, talk with the woman outside of the group time. Affirm her for her vulnerability and willingness to share and be prepared to refer her for more help if the need arises.

NOT SHARING AS MUCH AS THE OTHERS: If
you notice there is a woman who seems to not be as talkative as the others in the group, you may try gently asking for her input directly at some point in the conversation. Some women are naturally shyer than others; don't try to force them into an extroverted role, but do let them know their input is valuable to the group. Remind them of the goals of the study and how being vulnerable with one another is one of the ways God shapes us spiritually. If a woman is just not interested in being in the study and is holding the rest of the group back, meet with her outside the group setting to discuss her further involvement.

Keep in mind that no two women are alike, but keep the best interests of the group in mind as you lead. Encourage group members to follow the Ground Rules for Group Discussion Time (listed below and also found on pages 5–6 in the study guide.) Review these items together as often as needed in order to keep the conversation on track:

BE CONCISE

Share your answers to the questions while protecting others' time for sharing. Be thoughtful. Don't be afraid to share with the group, but try not to dominate the conversation.

KEEP GROUP MEMBERS' STORIES CONFIDENTIAL

Many things your group members share are things they are choosing to share with you, not with your husband or other friends. Protect each other by not allowing anything shared in the group to leave the group.

RELY ON SCRIPTURE FOR TRUTH

We are prone to use conventional, worldly wisdom as truth. While there is value in that, this is not the place. If you feel led to respond, please only respond with God's truth and Word, not "advice."

NO COUNSELING

Protect the group by not directing all attention on solving one person's problem. This is the place for confessing and discovery and applying truth together as a group. As a group leader, you will be able to direct a woman to more help outside the group time if she needs it.

WHEN TO REFER

Some of the women in your care may be suffering beyond the point you feel able to help. This study may bring the pain of circumstances or behaviors to the surface. To leave women in this state would be more damaging than helpful. Don't try to take on problems you do not feel equipped to handle. If you sense that a woman may need more help, follow up and refer her to someone.

:: Check with your church or pastor for names of trusted Christian counselors. Some major indicators of this need would be: depression, anxiety, thoughts of suicide, abuse, or a broken marriage. These are the obvious ones, but honestly, some women who are stuck in hurt from their past, minor depression, or fear could also benefit from counseling. I believe counseling is beneficial for many. So keep a stash of names for anyone you may feel needs to process further with a professional.

:: Look for the nearest Celebrate Recovery group and offer to attend the first meeting with her (www.celebraterecovery.com).

:: Suggest further resources and help to make a plan for their future growth and well-being.

:: Communicate with the leadership at your church about how to proceed with care.

:: Do not abandon these hurting women in a vulnerable place. This may be the first time they have opened up about painful hurts or patterns. Own their care and see it through. If they have landed in your group, God has assigned them to you for this season, until they are trusted to the care of someone else. Even then, continue to check in on them.

TYPES OF LEARNERS

Hopefully, you will be blessed to be leading this study with a group diverse in age, experience, and style. While the benefits of coming together as a diverse group to discuss God outweigh the challenges by a mile, there are often distinctions in learning styles. Just be aware and consider some of the differences in two types of learning styles that may be represented. (These are obviously generalizations, and each woman as an individual will express her own unique communication style, but in general these are common characteristics.)

Experiential Learners

These are women who are more transparent, don't like anything cheesy, want to go deep quickly, and are passionate. Make a safe environment for them by being transparent yourself and engaging their hearts. These women may not care as much about head knowledge and may care more deeply how knowledge about God applies to their lives. They want to avoid being put in a box. Keep the focus on applying truth to their lives and they will stay engaged.

Pragmatic Learners

These women are more accustomed to a traditional, inductive, or precept approach to Bible study. They have a high value for truth and authority but may not place as high a value on the emotional aspects of confessing sin and being vulnerable. To them it may feel unnecessary or dramatic. Keep the focus on the truth of Scripture. These women keep truth in the forefront of their lives and play a valuable role in discipleship.

✳ ✳ ✳

Because this study is different from traditional studies, some women may need more time to get used to the approach. The goal is still to make God big in our lives, to know and love him more, and to deal with sin by instructing with Scripture. These are the goals for all believers; we all just approach them in unique ways to reach unique types of people. I actually wrote this study praying it could reach both types of learners. I am one who lives with a foot in both worlds, trying to apply the deep truths I gained in seminary in an experiential way. I pray that this study would deeply engage the heart and the mind, and that we would be people who worship God in spirit and in truth, not just learning about sin but going to war with it together.

Common struggles like fear, stress, anger, shame, and insecurity are not respecters of age, religion, or income level. These struggles are human. But I have seen that as women are honest about them, we transcend the typical boundaries of Christian and seeker, young and old, single and married, needy and comfortable, coming together and to God in a unique and powerful way.

In the following pages and notes for each *Restless* lesson, I hope I have given you enough guidance that you do not feel lost, but enough freedom to depend on the Holy Spirit. These are only suggestions, but hopefully these notes will help surface themes and goals to guide you through your discussion of group members' homework and through the discussion of the Ask conversation cards. The video, homework, and cards should provide more than enough material for great discussions, but stay on track and be sure people are walking away with hope and truth.

Because you were made for more.

During this first meeting you will be getting to know each other, handing out the study guides, walking through the Instructions and Expectations (found on pages 4–10 of the study guide), walking through the Getting Started lesson (found on pages 11–30 of the study guide), and watching the first video.

Here are some general goals and thoughts for your time together this week:

:: Make the women feel safe.

:: Get to know each other and the things that are making you restless.

:: Set expectations for the study.

:: Have the people in your group go through the Respond section of the introductory lesson and discuss your responses.

:: Instruct group members on how to use the study guide and ASK Conversation Cards.

:: Reinforce that all of us are restless for something and that God wants us to live our everyday lives in light of eternity. But this is sometimes difficult to do.

:: Introduce Joseph on pages 12-14.

LEADER: This first session's suggested format is different from the others since it is your first meeting and there is no homework to review.

OPEN

Welcome your group warmly and enthusiastically. You set the tone for being open to the teaching and transformation available in this study. You can choose how to introduce people, but it is nice to get everyone on a first name basis before you jump in.

SEE—VIDEO TEACHING

For this first meeting, it is best to begin by watching video session one: INTRODUCTION :: RESTLESS (streaming or on DVD).

ASK—GROUP DISCUSSION TIME

1. Together take some time to read Instructions and Expectations and the Getting Started lesson in the study guide either aloud or to yourselves and discuss.

2. When you reach page 29 in the Getting Started lesson of the study guide, have participants choose the three things holding you back from dreaming. Give everyone time to think about this and write down in their guide their three things.

3. If you are in a large group, break into small groups and give each person the chance to open up about the three things keeping her from dreaming right now. Leaders, share first and be transparent.

4. After all the women have shared, transition to the Conversation Cards for discussion. The cards for this week are labeled "RESTLESS" on the front. Lead participants to choose, answer, and discuss the questions on the cards. (You can review the instructions for using the cards in ASK on page 220.) Close this discussion in prayer.

CLOSE

Read this week's Scripture memory verse aloud to the group and challenge the group to commit the verse to memory each week as best they can.

Let us throw off everything that hinders and the sin that so easily entangles. And let us run with perseverance the race marked out for us, fixing our eyes on Jesus, the pioneer and perfecter of faith . . . so that you will not grow weary and lose heart.

HEBREWS 12:1–3

Instruct the group to complete Session 2: GOD'S STORY Study and Projects before the next group meeting.

GOD'S STORY :: 2

The place where your restless soul meets God is the place where nothing ever feels small again.

MAIN IDEA: We were built to live for this eternal story, even in our everyday mundane lives. Often we forget the weight of the spiritual and miss how God wants us to participate.

This week we will be wrestling with our places in this very big story that God is building. Rather than feeling small in it, help your people to see that this is an honor to be a part of, and it could change the way we view every part of our lives.

Here are some general goals and thoughts for your time together this week:

:: Identify what is difficult to believe about God's story. Encourage open, honest sharing. We all doubt God at times.

:: Dream about how God's story could impact our day-to-day life.

:: Discuss God's love for us in this story. How does that change you?

:: Discuss how this story could and should affect our dreams and hopes for our time here.

MAIN GOAL: That you would be transformed by the story of God and compelled to live for the story of God.

OPEN—HOMEWORK DISCUSSION

Here are some suggested places to focus as you go over the homework together. Ask the group:

:: Share what you learned as you studied God's work on the earth in Hebrews 10:36–12:3.

:: How did John 17 speak to you based on where you are in your life right now?

:: Discuss your response to Projects 2 and 3.

:: What else did you learn as you studied and interacted with the lesson and Scripture this week?

SEE—VIDEO TEACHING

Watch video session two: GOD'S STORY

ASK—CONVERSATION CARDS

If you are in a large group, break into small groups of five for discussion time using the ASK: Conversation Cards. The cards for this week are labeled "GOD'S STORY." Remember to begin with the Scripture card and end by stressing the scriptural truth group members can apply to their lives as a result of what they discussed in your group time. Close this discussion in prayer.

CLOSE

Read this week's Scripture memory verse aloud to the group. Remind and challenge the group to commit these verses to memory each week as best they can.

> I have brought you glory on earth by finishing the work you gave me to do.
>
> **JOHN 17:4**

Encourage the group to complete Session 3: GIFTS Study and Projects before the next group meeting.

GIFTS :: 3

God has a plan to use your gifts, personality, and work
to display himself to your portion of the world.

MAIN IDEA: We each have unique gifts that God wants to reveal and unleash for his glory.

This week we studied the account of Joseph's dreams, and hopefully everyone gained new insight into this familiar story. God equipped Joseph with gifts that were part of his plan, and he has done the same for you.

Here are some general goals and thoughts for your time together this week:

:: Create a restlessness in the women, so that they don't settle for mediocre lives or wasted gifts.

:: Our motive for action must be the glory of God; create a burden in your group members for the glory of God on this earth.

:: What does it look like to live with a single-minded desire to see God and please him?

:: Understand that many of the moments in our lives we have felt most fulfilled likely contain our unique gifts and passions.

:: Identify the things that hold us back from using our gifts.

MAIN GOAL: Identify and name your gifts and dream about how you could use them.

OPEN—HOMEWORK DISCUSSION

Here are some suggested places to focus as you go over the homework together. Ask the group:

:: Discuss 1 Corinthians 13:1–12. Describe the attributes of love, and how a person's gifts come to life with such love.

:: What are you afraid might happen if you really use your gifts?

:: What was God speaking to you through 1 Corinthians 12?

:: Share your results from Project 4. Have people pair up so that every-one gets to share.

:: What else did you learn as you studied and interacted with the lesson and Scripture this week?

SEE—VIDEO TEACHING

Watch video session three: GIFTS

ASK—CONVERSATION CARDS

If you are in a large group, break into small groups of five for discussion time using the ASK: Conversation Cards. The cards for this week are labeled "GIFTS." Remember to begin with the Scripture card and end by stressing the scriptural truth group members can apply to their lives as a result of what they discussed in your group time. Close this discussion in prayer.

CLOSE

Read this week's Scripture memory verse aloud to the group and challenge the group to commit these verses to memory each week as best they can.

Just as a body, though one, has many parts, but all its many parts form one body, so it is with Christ.

1 CORINTHIANS 12:12

Close with prayer.

Encourage the group to complete Session 4: SUFFERING Study and Projects before the next group meeting.

SUFFERING :: 4

Out of our pain we could heal our world.

MAIN IDEA: That our sufferings could contain our deepest passions and the things we would most like to see healed around us.

This week we studied a potentially painful subject: suffering. We asked God to heal our hearts and show us the purpose behind our pain.

Here are some general goals and thoughts for your time together this week:

:: To accept, heal, and consider how God may want to move in and through our suffering.

:: To observe how Joseph served through and with his suffering.

:: To consider how our suffering has equipped and matured us.

MAIN GOAL: To uncover and process the moments that we have suffered most and consider how God may want to redeem that for others' healing.

OPEN—HOMEWORK DISCUSSION

Here are some suggested places to focus as you go over the homework together. Ask the group:

:: As you studied Joseph's suffering this week, what did you learn?

:: What did you uncover as you studied 2 Corinthians 1:3–7 this week?

:: Which project stood out to you most this week?

:: What else did you learn as you studied and interacted with the lesson and Scripture this week?

SEE—VIDEO TEACHING

Watch video session four: SUFFERING

ASK–CONVERSATION CARDS

If you are in a large group, break into small groups of five for discussion time using the ASK: Conversation Cards. The cards for this week are labeled "SUFFERING." Remember to begin with the Scripture card and end by stressing the scriptural truth group members can apply to their lives as a result of what they discussed in your group time. Close this discussion in prayer.

CLOSE

Read this week's Scripture memory verse aloud to the group and challenge the group to commit these verses to memory each week as best they can.

Praise be to the God and Father of our Lord Jesus Christ, the Father of compassion and the God of all comfort, who comforts us in all our troubles, so that we can comfort those in any trouble with the comfort we ourselves receive from God.

2 CORINTHIANS 1:3–4

Close with prayer.

Encourage the group to complete Session 5: PLACE Study and Projects before the next group meeting.

PLACES :: 5

It's not our places; it's what we do in our places.

MAIN IDEA: Places will never fulfill us, but can serve as the fertile ground for God to make himself known through us.

Here are some general goals and thoughts for your time together this week:

:: Our places are significant because God sets us in them and has work for us to do there.

:: Even so, there is freedom for God to move through us wherever we are.

:: Joseph received his places as God's will and worked hard for God's glory despite severe limitations and suffering.

:: It is not about where we are, but how we execute God's mission for our lives wherever we are.

:: If we would each fulfill God's work for our lives in our spots, the whole earth would be more full of his love and glory.

:: We will never be fully satisfied in any place, except our eternal home with God one day.

MAIN GOAL: Lead people to consider their places and what it would look like to live more intentionally in them.

OPEN—HOMEWORK DISCUSSION

Begin by reviewing the personal study from last week. Here are some suggested places to focus as you review:

:: Talk about Joseph's places in Genesis 39 and 40, and discuss his reactions to those places.

:: Look back at Philippians 1:12–26. What did you learn about place?

:: What kind of vision might God have for your places? Discuss Project 1.

:: What else did you learn as you studied and interacted with the lesson and Scripture this week?

SEE—VIDEO TEACHING

Watch video session five: PLACES

ASK—CONVERSATION CARDS

If you are in a large group, break into small groups of five for discussion time using the ASK: Conversation Cards. This cards for this week are labeled "PLACES." Remember to begin with the Scripture card and end by stressing the scriptural truth group members can apply to their lives as a result of what they discussed in your group time. Close this discussion in prayer.

CLOSE

Read this week's Scripture memory verse aloud to the group and challenge the group to commit these verses to memory each week as best they can.

For to me, to live is Christ and to die is gain.

PHILIPPIANS 1:21

Close with prayer.

Encourage the group to complete Session 6: PEOPLE Study and Projects before the next group meeting.

PEOPLE :: 6

GOD'S STORY

God's economy makes beautiful exchanges: as we give, we grow.

MAIN IDEA: When we run our races, there are people we need and people who need us.

Here are some general goals and thoughts for your time together this week:

:: We need people to encourage us as we run and to remind us of our bigger purposes.

:: We brush shoulders with people who need us, and God wants us to not waste time with them and opportunities to love them well wherever we are.

:: Intentional relationships take time and work and grace. Relationships often break down; it will take a lot of grace to stick with your people.

:: Our greatest purposes are often revealed by those who know us best, and through loving and meeting needs in the people around us.

MAIN GOAL: Identify the need for the right people in your life to help you run your race, and identify the people God has put on your path to love with his love.

OPEN—HOMEWORK DISCUSSION

Begin by reviewing the personal study from last week. Here are some suggested places to focus as you review::

:: What did you think of the way Joseph treats people in Genesis 41–45? What stood out about his behavior?

:: What convicted you in Hebrews 10:19–36?

:: Break into pairs and share your charts from Project 1 with each other.

:: What else did you learn as you studied and interacted with the lesson and Scripture this week?

SEE—VIDEO TEACHING

Watch video session six: PEOPLE

ASK—CONVERSATION CARDS

If you are in a large group, break into small groups of five for discussion time using the ASK: Conversation Cards. The cards for this week are labeled "PEOPLE." Remember to begin with the Scripture card and end by stressing the scriptural truth group members can apply to their lives as a result of what they discussed in your group time. Close this discussion in prayer.

CLOSE

Read this week's Scripture memory verse aloud to the group and challenge the group to review their memory verses to date and continue committing each verse to memory as best they can.

Put on then, as God's chosen ones, holy and beloved, compassionate hearts, kindness, humility, meekness, and patience, bearing with one another and, if one has a complaint against another, forgiving each other; as the Lord has forgiven you, so you also must forgive. And above all these put on love, which binds everything together in perfect harmony. And let the peace of Christ rule in your hearts, to which indeed you were called in one body. And be thankful.

COLOSSIANS 3:12–15 ESV

Close with prayer.

Encourage the group to complete Session 7: PASSIONS Study and Projects before the next group meeting.

PASSIONS :: 7

God built us to love different things so
we could meet different needs.

MAIN IDEA: God often leads us to passions through suffering experienced or perceived.

Here are some general goals and thoughts for your time together this week:

:: Passions are the needs you see around you or around the world that uniquely make your heart race or move you.

:: We are most fulfilled when we are meeting needs around us.

:: God prepared good works in advance for us to walk in. Dream about what those could be.

:: It is a privilege to participate in the work of God. What is holding you back?

:: There are two big passion killers: comparison and fear of man's approval. What does it look like to be free of those?

MAIN GOAL: To identify unique need that you are designed to meet and be moved by God to meet it.

OPEN—HOMEWORK DISCUSSION

Begin by reviewing the personal study from last week. Here are some suggested places to focus as you review:

:: What did you learn by studying Joseph's passions this week?

:: How did your view of the word *passion* change this week?

:: What passions arose in you as you worked through Project 1?

:: From Project 2, what does it look like to fight comparison and the fear of man?

:: What else did you learn as you studied and interacted with the lesson and Scripture this week?

SEE—VIDEO TEACHING

Watch video session seven: PASSIONS

ASK—CONVERSATION CARDS

If you are in a large group, break into small groups of five for discussion time using the ASK: Conversation Cards. The cards for this week are labeled "PASSIONS." Remember to begin with the Scripture card and end by stressing the scriptural truth group members can apply to their lives as a result of what they discussed in your group time. Close this discussion in prayer.

CLOSE

Read this week's Scripture memory verse aloud to the group and challenge the group to review their memory verses to date and continue committing each verse to memory as best they can.

For the joy set before him he endured the cross, scorning its shame, and sat down at the right hand of the throne of God. Consider him who endured such opposition from sinners, so that you will not grow weary and lose heart.

HEBREWS 12:2–3

Close with prayer.

Encourage the group to complete Session 8: MYSTERY Study and Projects before the next group meeting.

MYSTERY :: 8

Nothing we have done matters without the Spirit of God.

MAIN IDEA: God's goal for our lives is that we would live in complete and utter surrender and dependence on him. He built us to need him. So our purposes are most likely fleshed out and revealed and lived moving closely with his Spirit.

Here are some general goals and thoughts for your time together this week:

:: Lean into what you don't know as much as what you do know. God is in this with us. He doesn't reveal every detail of our lives, or we would not depend on him so desperately.

:: He often moves through our weakness and fear more than our strength and confidence.

:: The Spirit can move powerfully through the very most average of us.

:: Life is best lived in relationship with Jesus: eyes fixed, heart simply in love with him and moved to obey him no matter the costs.

:: None of our threads are all the same, which means we each must feel tremendous responsibility to steward our lives—and the threads God has given us—well.

MAIN GOAL: No matter what we know or don't know about our purposes, God is most after us in relationship with him.

OPEN—HOMEWORK DISCUSSION

Begin by reviewing the personal study from last week. Here are some suggested places to focus as you review:

:: As you studied the scriptures this week, what stood out to you?

:: As you look through the threads of your life, what stands out to you?

:: Break up into pairs and let your partner share what she sees as she studies the unique threads God has given her.

:: Share how your perspective has shifted since the first week.

SEE—VIDEO TEACHING

Watch video session eight: MYSTERY

ASK—CONVERSATION CARDS

If you are in a large group, break into small groups of five for discussion time using the ASK: Conversation Cards. The cards for this final week's discussion are labeled "MYSTERY." Remember to begin with the Scripture card and end by stressing the scriptural truth group members can apply to their lives as a result of what they discussed in your group time.

CLOSE

Share your personal experience you've had in these weeks together. Allow the group to share similar stories. If a member of your group is having difficulty with the study coming to a close or facing anxiety about what might be next for them, take a moment to surround them and pray for them.

Read this week's Scripture memory verse aloud to the group and remind the group to go back through all the memory verses from weeks one through seven. Encourage them to keep committing these verses to memory as they allow themselves to embrace the greater story God has for their lives—these verses will guide them and lead them well.

But the Advocate, the Holy Spirit, whom the Father will send in my name, will teach you all things and will remind you of everything I have said to you.

JOHN 14:26

Identify the Threads of Your Life

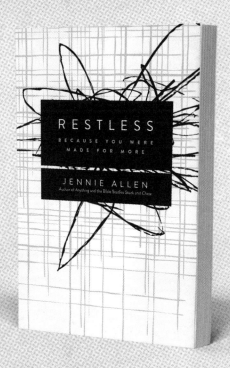

Using the story of Joseph, Jennie explains how his suffering, gifts, story, and relationships fit into the greater story of God—and how your story can do the same. She introduces Threads—a tool to help you see your own personal story and to uncover and understand the raw materials God has given you to use for his glory and purpose.

Available wherever books & Bibles are sold.

NO MORE PRETENDING. NO MORE PERFORMING.
NO MORE FIGHTING TO PROVE YOURSELF.

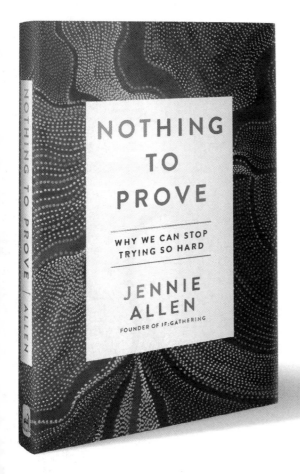

Are you scared that God doesn't have enough for you today, that you have to muster it up on your own? Are you tired from trying to be more than who you are? Discover the joy of resting in God's delight in you. Discover the joy of having nothing to prove.

Available everywhere books are sold.

"Feelings were never meant to be fixed; feelings are meant to be felt."

JENNIE ALLEN

Exchange stuffing, dismissing, or minimizing your emotions for a ***five-step process*** to know what you feel and what to do about it.

LEARN MORE: JENNIEALLEN.COM

WATERBROOK

You are in charge of your thoughts.
They are not in charge of you.

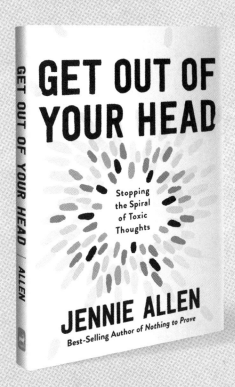

Get Out of Your Head: Stopping the Spiral of Toxic Thoughts is a Biblical guide to discovering how to submit our minds to Christ because how we think shapes how we live. As we surrender every thought to Jesus, the promises of God flood our lives in profound ways.

Visit **getoutofyourheadbook.com** for info about *Get Out of Your Head.*

Available wherever books are sold.

We Aren't Supposed to Be This Lonely.

But you don't have to stay there. Let's find your people.

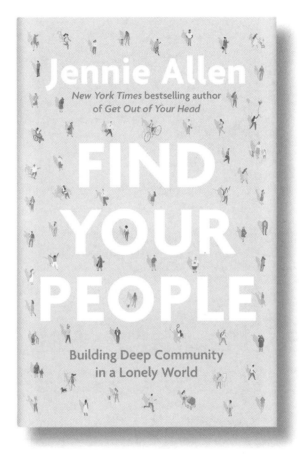

You were created to play, engage, adventure, and explore—with others. In *Find Your People*, you'll discover exactly how to dive into the deep end and experience the full wonder of community. Because while the ache of loneliness is real, it doesn't have to be your reality.

WATERBROOK

waterbrookmultnomah.com

ALSO AVAILABLE FROM JENNIE ALLEN

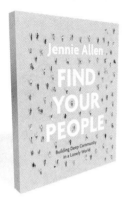

BUILDING DEEP COMMUNITY IN A LONELY WORLD

This seven-session video Bible study looks at the original community in Genesis and the Trinity to see how God intended for us to live in community all along.

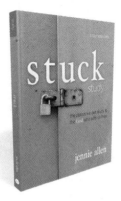

IDENTIFY THE THREADS OF YOUR LIFE

Stuck is an eight-session video Bible study leading women to the invisible struggles that we fight and to the God who has to set us free.

STOPPING THE SPIRAL OF TOXIC THOUGHTS

In this six-session, video Bible study, Jennie inspires and equips us to transform our emotions, our outlook, and even our circumstances by taking control of our thoughts.

WHAT THE BIBLE TELLS US ABOUT OUR EMOTIONS

This six-session video Bible study teaches how your emotions actually help you notice what's wrong and connect with God and others more deeply.

YOU ARE ENOUGH BECAUSE JESUS IS ENOUGH.

In this eight-session video Bible study, Jennie Allen walks through key passages in the Gospel of John that demonstrate how Jesus is enough. We don't have to prove anything because Jesus has proven everything.

CHASING AFTER THE HEART OF GOD

Chase is an eight-session video Bible study experience to discover the heart of God and what it is exactly He wants from us through major events in the life of David and the Psalms.

Visit JennieAllen.com for more info. Available wherever books & Bibles are sold.